BEHIND THE COUCH

BEHIND THE COUCH

REVELATIONS OF A PSYCHOANALYST

Herbert S. Strean
As told to Lucy Freeman

WILEY

JOHN WILEY & SONS

New York · Chichester · Brisbane · Toronto · Singapore

Library of Congress Cataloging-in-Publication Data:
Strean, Herbert S.
     Behind the couch.
     1. Psychoanalysis—Case studies.   2. Psychotherapist
and patient.   3. Psychoanalysts.   I. Freeman, Lucy.
II. Title.   [DNLM: 1. Psychoanalysis—personal narratives.
WZ 100 S914]
RC504.S784   1988   616.89'17   88-274
ISBN 0-471-85956-7

*To Reuben Fine, Ph.D., in gratitude for his
creation of "the analytic ideal"*

ACKNOWLEDGMENTS

We wish to thank Herb Reich, senior editor at John Wiley & Sons, for his constant stimulation, constructive criticism, generous support, and inspiring direction, as well as his sense of humor;

Judith Overton, Mr. Reich's assistant, for her constant availability and devotion, both to us and to the cause of psychoanalysis, way beyond the call of duty;

Marcia Strean, for going over several drafts of the manuscript and coming up with excellent suggestions;

Richard and Billy Strean, Dr. Strean's severest critics, for constantly prodding their father to rethink his role as an analyst and to ponder what psychoanalysis can and cannot do;

And the many pseudonymous patients discussed here, without whom there would be no book.

Finally, the authors wish to acknowledge their gratitude to each other for work on the three other books on which they have collaborated: *Freud and Women*; *Guilt: Letting Go*; and *Raising Cain: How to Help Your Children Achieve a Happy Sibling Relationship.* Lucy Freeman's book, *Fight against Fears*, was the first to be written by a patient about a complete psychoanalysis. *Behind the Couch* is the first book in which a psychoanalyst reveals his own thoughts, feelings, fantasies, and memories as he sat listening to patients over the years—the first book about how an analyst feels as he sits behind the couch.

H. S. S.

L. F.

CONTENTS

CONTENTS

BEHIND THE COUCH

INTRODUCTION

For over a quarter of a century I have been a psychoanalyst. During these years, just about every patient I've treated has displayed an intense curiosity about my life. This is not unique to me; it happens to every psychoanalyst.

Since the start of psychoanalysis in 1891, when the first patient lay down on Freud's couch, patients and nonpatients alike have shown a deep curiosity about psychoanalysts. They want to know what an analyst thinks and feels as he sits behind the couch, listening all day and sometimes well into the night to the woes of troubled patients.

What kind of person is the psychoanalyst? How does he behave with his wife, his children, his parents, his mother-in-law, his siblings? Was *he* traumatized in childhood? Did he choose the profession of psychoanalysis so he could work out his own neurotic problems? Does he feel superior to his patients? What were his *real* motives in becoming an analyst?

Does the analyst become sexually aroused when a patient tries to seduce him? Does he become furious when a patient accuses him of being stupid or despicable? Or unappealing and asexual?

1

What is it about human suffering that interests him? Is he a sadist who gets gratification from listening all day, every day of the working week, to tales of the suffering of others? Is he a voyeur who craves knowledge of the sexual fantasies and practices of his patients? What is *his* sexual life like? Does he get sexual pleasure and gratification? Does he ever express anger in his own home? Does he lose his temper at wife and children?

What of the analyst's own personal analysis? What sort of patient was—or is—he? Does he still suffer from unresolved conflicts? Will they affect his patients? These and other questions seem to haunt a great many people.

Why are so many men and women curious about analysts? Why do they sometimes mask their curiosity with caustic humor? Cartoons regularly portray the analyst as a hostile, bearded man. A popular joke involves a young analyst in training who worriedly asks a seasoned analyst, "How can you bear to listen day after day, hour after hour, to such torment and suffering?" To which the older analyst replies, "Who listens?" This joke implies that the analyst is a fraud. It also gives the teller and the listener a temporary outlet for their fear of and hostility toward the professional who has declared himself an expert on such matters as sex, aggression, dreams, fantasies and memories—dimensions of life that most people wish to avoid thinking too deeply about.

Ask an analyst about his personal life or feelings and he will probably say, "Let's find out why you want to know," or "What are your fantasies about this?" Because he avoids answering questions about himself, he remains mysterious. He is close-mouthed about his way of life, his values, and even his feelings, rarely discussing these dimensions of his existence in public, much less in print. Some analysts even believe they should not support or protest social and political causes because in doing so they might violate their anonymity.

Many other professionals, including lawyers, ministers, and doctors, feel free to reveal why they chose their work—but not analysts. Consequently, the public knows the least about psychoanalysts, yearns to know more about them. Yet, it has often been surprising to me to note how infrequently analysts write or talk about their reactions to their work.

If the analyst did not sit behind the couch and remain unseen, perhaps there wouldn't be so much curiosity about him. Maybe this unseen aspect stirs up the wish to know. Because he is invisible to the patient, says few words and rarely if ever talks about himself, the analyst's very elusiveness stimulates speculation. The patient wonders about what the analyst's face expresses. Is he in deep concentration about the patient or is his mind elsewhere? Is he, horror of horrors, falling asleep or yawning? Or is he taking notes?

Another reason the patient is so curious about the analyst is that he symbolizes the patient's parents of childhood, stirs up childhood curiosity about secrets, especially sexual secrets between the parents. What went on between mother and father behind those closed doors?

People are curious about the thoughts and the private lives of public figures, who are sometimes viewed as parental models. It is no coincidence that the bedroom arrangements of every president of the United States are made public at some time during his tenure in office. We know President Gerald Ford and his wife, Betty, slept in the same bedroom, and that John and Jacqueline Kennedy had separate rooms, as did Richard and Patricia Nixon. Such information is of interest to the public because important people become parental figures—and everybody fantasizes what takes place when the doors close behind them at night.

The public seems equally curious about the private lives of other famous people, including athletes. A baseball or football player who appears on television will usually reveal his marital status and the number of children he has, as well as how he feels about his fellow players and the manager or owner of the team. He may even write his autobiography, as movie stars, politicians, and successful corporation heads do.

Why, then, is the analyst so secretive? What makes him different?

One important reason, essential to all therapy, keeps the analyst silent about his personal life: he must remain essentially anonymous so as to help the patient. The patient's past—*his* fantasies, wishes, behavior—has to emerge, and the patient has to understand that past in terms of his life alone. If the analyst talks about himself, he interferes with—seriously blocks—the flow of the patient's thoughts as he free associates. The treatment is damaged, sometimes beyond repair, if the therapist intrudes with details of his life.

Perhaps the most important dimension of psychoanalysis is the close study of what analysts call the "transference." This encompasses the way the patient feels toward the analyst as he slowly revives in memory the loves, hatreds and ambivalences of his childhood. He "transfers" the wishes, fantasies, and behavior of the past to the analyst, his current target of emotional outlet. If the analyst becomes anything but a listener and interpreter, he is not fulfilling his role as helper but is, instead, interfering with the process of psychoanalysis.

The analyst helps the patient examine how he emotionally experiences the analyst as his mother and father of childhood. The patient then becomes free to understand how he has distorted many of his childhood memories and experiences and both overidealized and overhated his parents at times. In this way, he comes to terms with his irrational fantasies and unresolved conflicts. He realizes how they may have crippled his sense of self and his awareness of reality.

Thus the analyst, by remaining essentially anonymous, helps the patient discover how he has related to the important persons in his life, past and present, in ways that have been emotionally harmful. By divulging information about himself, the analyst would be denying the patient his right to know only about himself, and this would inhibit the process of the discovery of the inner self.

Freud warned analysts against revealing anything personal. He referred to the analyst as "a mirror" reflecting to the patient his conflicts and feelings. But sometimes Freud ignored his own warning. We know only a limited amount about his personal life yet he was one of the most revelatory of analysts—most of the dreams he reported in books were his own.

Not so the analyst of the 1980s. Many times I have joined analytic colleagues at a party, on a golf course, or at dinner, and even in these relaxed settings I've found them quite unresponsive to personal questions. Once, as a party was ending, I offered a ride to a colleague. "Do you have transportation?" I asked.

He replied, "Why do you ask?"

I said, "I just thought you might want a lift home."

He then asked, "What's your motive for offering me a lift?"—as if I were lying on the couch and he was analyzing me.

When psychoanalysis first began, Freud was much influenced by the medical model in which the patient was "sick" and the analyst was "healthy." Many analysts still regard the patient and the analyst as two struggling human beings—one "sick," the other "healthy"—trying together to fathom the mysteries of psychic life. The "healthy" one, in this model, never has to reveal himself; the "sick" one must tell all he can about himself. Unfortunately, this model is still in vogue.

Freud probably found it difficult to view psychoanalysis as a mutual relationship between two participants because he himself had not been analyzed. Later practitioners were analyzed before practicing, and they knew how it felt to be a patient. I believe, however, it has been very difficult for most analysts to talk about being a patient and to experience themselves in the patient role. I think they try very hard to distance themselves, to avoid feeling like a patient and identifying with the patient.

There is ample support for this belief. Freud in 1910 introduced the idea of "countertransference"—the subjective, personal feelings and fantasies the analyst possesses toward the patient. But not until May 4, 1984, did the American Psychoanalytic Association raise the subject of countertransference at one of its annual meetings. That seventy-four-year delay reflects the reluctance of analysts to discuss this topic.

Freud tended to regard countertransference as an impediment to analytic work, and many analysts still subscribe to this point of view. But within the last few years countertransference has been viewed as an inevitable, ubiquitous aspect of the analytic process and an important source of information for the analyst about both the patient and himself.

For many years I have felt that unless I could permit myself to free associate to my patient's expressed thoughts and words and constantly explore what I was feeling in the analytic process, I could not really be of much help to the patient. If the analyst cannot put himself in the patient's shoes and feel the patient's anger, dependency, and sexual fantasies, he becomes, in my opinion, a mere mechanic rather than a feeling human being trying to help another human being who is suffering deep psychic pain.

The analyst has to be constantly aware of the feelings of the patient, react silently to what the patient is feeling and saying, and, out of this morass of emotions and words, offer a few ideas to help the patient. The analyst must also be invulnerable, at least as far as expressing himself is concerned, to verbal assaults and protestations of undying love.

One patient may tell him he's the most understanding, tolerant, wise, empathic soul in the world. A second patient may accuse him of being the most unempathic, unfeeling scoundrel alive. Another will insist he wants to remain in analysis with him for the rest of his life. Still another will angrily threaten to leave the blasted couch at once and never return.

As the analyst experiences this wide range of human emotions, he reacts with a wide range of emotions. Yet no analyst has written of what he subjectively feels or thinks when a patient praises or attacks him.

One of my main purposes in writing this book is to show that the psychoanalyst is fundamentally a human being. I believe many men and women shun psychoanalytic treatment because they are afraid to embark on an intimate relationship with an unfeeling analyst, an automaton. As I share my anxieties, elation, and irritation, perhaps those men and women will understand that psychoanalysis is nothing more and nothing less than a human relationship between two struggling human beings who are similar in many ways.

Let's face it: psychoanalysts eat, sleep, go to the bathroom, experience feelings of love and hate, elation and depression, are political, social, and intellectual human beings just like everyone else—even though many of them seem reluctant to admit that patients and analysts are created equal. Some analysts act like gods, but then, every analytic patient *wants* his analyst to be a god. Where does this wish come from and why is it so universal?

When an infant is a few months old, he slowly starts to realize he cannot have everything he wants at the very moment he wants it. As it dawns on him he is not a god, cannot control the world around him, he feels helpless and angry. To defend against this helplessness and anger, he fantasies his mother and father as the gods he would like to be. This fantasy continues through much of childhood.

It is more than a coincidence that many men and women speak of "Our Father who art in Heaven." Though now that we live in a society working toward women's equality, I have heard God referred to as "Our Mother who art in Heaven."

All of us feel less than perfect—because we are. All of us feel vulnerable, because the human condition is a vulnerable one. All of us want more than we possess—more love, more money, more prestige.

Because every human being feels limited and *is* limited, he seeks someone who will make his life as perfect as possible. Men and women who go to a psychoanalyst hope he will be in the image of a perfect parent who can restore to them the lost paradise of infancy.

I also believe that the analyst's insistence on remaining out of sight, just as God remains out of sight, probably enhances the fantasy of the analyst as a god. During my own personal analysis I could hear myself sounding like a child praying to God to make me into a perfect human being—a superman. If patients wish to be supermen, this means they fantasy their analysts as supermen. And I believe patients wish to see the analyst as a deity who should remain unknown.

And just as children feel upset when they realize their parents have limitations and vulnerabilities, are not gods, patients become upset when they realize their analysts are not perfect. I might therefore hypothesize that another reason the inner life of the psychoanalyst has been shrouded in secrecy is that an unconscious mutual pact exists between patient and analyst. The patient wants to keep the analyst an unseen, all-powerful god, and the analyst wishes to be experienced as that god.

When you sit behind the couch, there is a time to talk and a time to keep silent. Now, I like to talk, and I sometimes find it very difficult to keep quiet and listen. If I err, I err on the side of talking too much rather than keeping quiet for too long. When I was a young analyst, one of my supervisors suggested that I get drunk, go to work with a hangover, and be forced to remain silent with patients and see how much therapeutic progress would take place. Though I never took this advice, I did learn to keep quiet, and I discovered my patients felt better and functioned better. But I still find it hard to remain silent. When a patient tells me I'm the most wonderful person in the world, I want to say, "Thank you very much." When a patient calls me an inadequate jerk or an impotent schmuck, I want to say, "Why can't you see me as I am?" or "How ungrateful can you be? I'm only trying to help you."

Most patients will feel less troubled and develop greater self-esteem if they have an empathic listener who gives them the message, "Say whatever comes to mind. No matter what it is, I will love you and try to understand you." This is what psychologist Carl Rogers called "unconditional positive regard" and is an appropriate attitude for the psychoanalyst.

In daily life, when you bring your problems to a friend or relative, he usually gives quick advice, offers some reassurance, then talks about himself and what he would do in similar circumstances. He rarely listens quietly. It takes most psychoanalysts years to fully appreciate that quiet listening is one of the most important contributions they can offer.

However, I believe that keeping quiet and listening has something to do with the high rate of heart attacks among analysts. They have to keep their anger, irritation, and sexual responses to themselves as they silently encourage the patient to express more fully his anger, irritation, and sexual wishes. The analyst is supposed to have no reaction when he is the recipient of intense love, hatred, dependency, sexuality.

It has been my impression over the years that analysts consider it a sin to admit they are pleased when a patient loves them, upset when he hates them, irritated when the patient becomes dependent on them, and stimulated when the patient describes his sexual fantasies about the analyst. Perhaps if more analysts acknowledged their feelings to themselves, their incidence of heart attacks would be lower.

Because the analyst's fantasies and fears in the analytic situation have remained so secret, few people really know what makes an analyst tick. I have never read an article in the analytic literature that asks, "Why does someone select a profession where, all day long, he is exposed to mental suffering?" Analysts have written articles about the psychodynamics of artists, musicians, Wall Street financiers, and actors, but they have not examined the dynamics of the analyst—a person who is fascinated with emotional conflicts and psychic misery. Though analysts would be the first to speak of the voyeurism of an obstetrician or gynecologist, who looks at naked bodies all day, they do not discuss the voyeuristic pleasure they derive as they peer at people who are emotionally naked on the couch. The analysts sit in silence behind the patient, watching him and hearing him as he pours out his heart. How different is that from looking through a peephole at someone stripping off his clothes?

Human suffering has fascinated me for a variety of reasons all the way from altruism to, perhaps, perversity. When I work with patients and hear of their misery, temporarily I become them, feel their conflicts, empathize with them. Because I have been there, too, I can help them see how and why they arrange their own misery, eventually help them overcome it.

Altruism is easy to talk about. Most people who help others say they are interested in enhancing the lives of those they help. But this is an incomplete explanation of their motives. If analysts are really truthful they would also have to acknowledge a certain superiority that surfaces and says in essence to a patient, "I'm glad I'm not you. I feel stronger and more competent in facing life." If the analyst's need to feel superior is strong and is conveyed in any way to the patient, this can have a detrimental effect on the analysis. There is also the opposite feeling: many times I have said to myself as I listened to a patient, "There but for the grace of God lie I." Or from time to time I have envied some patients who appeared sharper and more insightful than I.

When an analyst is not able to help a patient, he usually is trying to deny in himself the very problem the patient presents. One way of denying a problem in yourself is to say, "Oh, how that poor patient suffers." Whenever I find myself feeling smug or superior, I ask myself what purpose this feeling serves for me. Usually I am warding off the very distress the patient is describing.

I believe most, though not all, analytic failures are related to the analyst's inability or reluctance to face in himself the very issue with which the patient is struggling. I have often thought that what an analyst considers "untreatable" is something he has not been able to resolve fully in himself. In my early days as an analyst I was not very successful with homosexual male patients. But when I began to acknowledge homosexual fantasies—my wishes as a little boy to cling to my father, my competition with my younger sister and my mother for his love—I could be much more compassionate and helpful to my homosexual patients.

Though the analyst must withhold many of his emotional reactions from the patient, he is a better therapist, I believe, if he permits himself to feel his own sexual, aggressive, and omnipotent wishes and even his emotional impotency at times.

The analyst's major strength in helping people is to know his own psyche, his own unconscious, his own past and present conflicts. They influence everything he says and does with a patient. In the chapters ahead I will try honestly to share what I felt and what I fantasied, what was conflict-free or conflictual in my work with a variety of patients. I will attempt to show the truth of one of my favorite quotations by the psychoanalyst Dr. Harry Stack Sullivan: "We are all more human than otherwise."

Before writing this book, I discussed the idea with my analytic colleagues and received the same response over and over: "It's the greatest idea I've ever heard of. It's courageous of you to want to do it. The field really needs such a book—but I could never do it." Virtually all my colleagues confessed they did not want anyone, particularly their patients, to know about their personal lives. They claimed their patients would be "very upset" to learn, for instance, that their analyst felt angry or frustrated or wanted to laugh or did not know an answer.

I have also been told by my colleagues that sharing my personal life is inappropriate, will create hazards in my work with current and future patients. Whether this is a projection of the fear other analysts have at revealing their feelings or whether it has elements of truth remains to be seen. I have thought of these admonitions carefully. For many years I had reservations about writing this book. But as I analyzed my reservations I came up with a few thoughts I believe important.

First, I realized my reservations related to my inhibitions and had little relation to my patients. I found that when patients read something I wrote or saw me outside the consultation room, they tended to use these experiences in their own unique way, perceiving me in terms of their current transference position. I wrote about this discovery in "The Extra-Analytic Contact," an article in *The Psychoanalytic Quarterly*, 1982.

Second, I feel that my main motive for writing this book is to show the psychoanalyst as a human being with strengths, eccentricities, whims, and weaknesses. I have been concerned about the stereotyping of analysts, rarely seen as they really are by the public. I hope this book will help educate the public so patients can more easily accept the fact they are working with a human being, not a god. I also hope it will enable troubled men and women to feel less afraid of psychoanalysts.

Third, this book evolves from the fact that, like all analysts, I spend most of my time empathically listening and trying to understand the lives of my patients. During the course of a day I can go for hours without saying a word. As a result, I have a powerful desire to communicate and talk to my readers who, over the years, have been like analysts to me—I do all the talking, they must listen (read).

This book is my way of communicating to readers, hoping they will find here and there a few words that may help them understand their lives more fully. This is not the same as being in analysis. But a glimmer of insight from the printed page can often help the reader delve deeper into what may be a puzzling conflict.

Few laymen appreciate how much strain there is on the analyst, who must constantly put himself in the other person's shoes—feel his feelings, identify with his conflicts, relive his memories, experience his dreams—and be quiet most of the time.

All patients overidealize the analyst to some extent, as they did their mother and father in childhood, a fantasy common to all of us. But parents are not gods. There are no gods. I have also written this book to help current and future patients say, "There are no gods before me—or behind me."

I hope I show this in the thirteen cases that follow.‡

---

‡ While the essential characteristics of the patients discussed in this book remain true to the facts, their names and certain distinguishing features have been changed to protect their privacy.

1

"WHO LISTENS?"
The Woman Who
Refused to Talk

I opened the door of my consultation room to face a petite young woman, red hair flowing to her shoulders. She wore a drab October outfit—slacks, sweater, and blouse—all in a sad brown shade. Her pale face held a depressed look that kept her from looking as attractive as she could have, I thought.

"Please come in, Mrs. Winthrop," I said.

She had been referred to me by her brother-in-law, a psychologist. He told me she had severe marital problems, but he didn't elaborate on their nature. I agreed to see her in consultation, to decide if I could treat her and to see if she wanted to work with me. She had called and asked for an appointment in a voice I could hardly hear.

Now she stood at the door of my consultation room, where I spend almost as much time as I do at home. It is a comfortable room, a quiet room; nothing in it is intrusive. Yet it is also a cheerful room, with north-facing windows through which the morning sun streams, unless I draw the beige drapes so the patient can concentrate on his internal world. The drapes at each side, from ceiling to floor, hide five shelves stacked with psychoanalytic journals.

My office is on the fifth floor of a building in New York City near Central Park West in the nineties. Only the First Church of Christ Scientist lies between my office and Central Park. At the moment of Mary Winthrop's appearance, the park held a profusion of reds, oranges, yellows and fading greens, autumn's colorful palette. The street on which my office is located has been called Libido Lane because a number of pioneer psychoanalysts have lived and worked on it: Dr. Berta Bornstein, Dr. Margaret Mahler, and Dr. Ralph Crowley, a founder of the William Alanson White Institute, which lies farther south on the park.

As Mrs. Winthrop surveyed what she undoubtedly thought of as my lair, she saw, in front of the windows to the right, my desk. On it, hidden from the gaze of patients, are a number of photographs of people important in my life—my wife Marcia; my two sons, Richard and Billy, now postgraduate students; Reuben Fine, founder of the New York Center for Psychoanalytic Training, of which I am now director; my father, Lyon P. Strean, Ph.D., a bacteriologist; and my uncle, George J. Strean, M.D., an obstetrician and gynecologist (I grew up thinking Labor was a town, so often did I hear my uncle say, "There's a woman in labor I have to see").

On the right-hand side of the room are two chairs and a round table that holds a large impressionistic sculpture, *Mother and Child*, appropriate to analytic treatment, I thought when I bought it. The mother, of black marble, and the baby, of white marble, are entwined. Two chairs, one on either side of the table, I use to supervise analytic students or for the occasional patient who prefers to sit up, instead of lying on the couch. Over the table hang three colorful prints of Paris, bought by my wife when we visited that city, which I thought added color to the room in a quiet way.

Against the opposite wall, the patient sees the couch, facing the windows. Beside it stands a small table holding tissues, within easy reach of the patient, to stem the many tears that flow. A second table stands between the back of the couch and my dark brown leather chair and hassock; this table holds my telephone and answering machine.

As I sit in the chair, to my left on the wall hangs a copy of a sensitive and moving portrait of Freud, sketched in 1926 by Professor Ferdinand Schmutzer, a neighbor in Vienna. Freud's eloquent brown eyes seem to show the sorrow within himself and all mankind, a plea for the understanding of the troubled self. At this time of life he was slightly balding, with white hair, white beard, white mustache. Also on the wall are my doctoral degree from Columbia University and an analytic certificate from the Society for Psychoanalytic Training, so patients can know where I have trained—all patients should make sure their analyst is qualified. Nearby is a painting of a farmhouse, given to me by a student I supervised. The scene is somewhat mystical, and it reminds me of Montreal, where I lived as a boy.

Behind my chair is the door through which the patient enters the room. On either side of it are floor-to-ceiling shelves filled with psychoanalytic books. Atop one bookcase stands a photograph of Dr. Theodor Reik, founder of the National Psychological Association for Psychoanalysis, where I received my psychoanalytic training after graduating in 1953 from the School of Social Work of Boston University. Reik sent this photograph to me in 1960, inscribed "To Herb Strean," and I cherish it. Both Freud and Reik, at least in spirit, are my constant companions in this room where I work long hours, often well into the evening.

All this Mary Winthrop could have seen as she first entered the room. But she seemed unaware of her surroundings, as are many patients when they first enter. She made no attempt to walk farther into the room, as though it held the horrors of hell, but stood in silence at the door.

I thought, as I looked at what she wore, that the colors a woman selects tell something about her. If she dresses in red, blue, yellow, orange, green, or purple, she seems cheerful. But if, like Mary Winthrop, she drapes herself in blacks, browns, and beiges, she usually feels depressed, perhaps mourning present or past losses. Mary's monochromatic brown clothing was relieved only by the red of her hair.

She wore no makeup, not even lipstick to give color. She was so slim I wondered if she were anorexic. She could not be called pretty, or even attractive, I thought, because she seemed so depressed. Perhaps after treatment, when she liked herself more and felt happier, she would appear attractive. I remember what Paul Federn, a famous analyst of Freud's day, said to women patients: "I can't promise you too much, but I can promise that you'll be prettier." With more acceptance of herself—her fantasies, her sexuality, her buried anger—Mary would look livelier, more winsome. Men and women seem younger, more appealing, happier, with the dawn of self-acceptance, as the worried, taut, depressed expressions leave their faces.

I gestured toward the two chairs to our right. Mary gingerly sat on one. I took the other, between us the sculpture of *Mother and Child.* I waited for her to speak. She had said not one word.

Still, she said nothing; she just stared at me with almost no expression in the brown eyes, which, when they gained some semblance of emotion, I thought, might be eloquent. I sensed that, for her, talking to me was going to be an arduous task.

I broke the silence. "Perhaps you could tell me what brings you here."

"I'm not very happy." It was all she could get out, her voice barely audible.

Another long silence.

I dared a second question. "Can you tell me some of the things in your life that make you feel unhappy?"

She allowed herself two words: "My marriage."

At least this was a communication, and an important one.

When she called for a consultation, she'd told me she was twenty-two years old, an artist of sorts, and married to a thirty-year-old stockbroker who could afford the seven-room apartment in which they lived on upper Park Avenue.

"How long have you been married, Mrs. Winthrop?"

"Three months." She lowered her brown eyes and looked at the floor, as though she were ashamed of the marriage.

Then, to my surprise, she suddenly offered, "I can't have sex."

"What stops you?"

"I don't know. As soon as my husband comes near me, wants to be intimate, I feel nauseated. Then I break out in hives. Sometimes I run to the bathroom and vomit. Or I have a bowel movement."

I waited for her to go on, pleased she was talking. It seemed to be an effort for her; sometimes I had to lean toward her to catch the words.

She sighed, then said, "We went through a courtship of six months that was only friendly. There was very little touching, holding, or kissing. I felt comfortable with that."

She retreated into another long silence. Heartened by her few words, I said, "Tell me something about your parents." She was a young woman; her mother and father should be alive.

Almost a whisper, "My mother died of cancer when I was six. I was the oldest of three daughters. My father expected me to take over my mother's work. I had to clean the house, shop for food, cook the meals, all the while trying to get high marks in school. I did get some help from Aunt Susan, my mother's sister. She lived down the street."

19

Mary had obviously been pushed and pressured to become a woman very early in life, I thought, never allowed to enjoy childhood. This meant important stages in her emotional development had been blocked and she would, as an adult, feel unfulfilled, depressed, mourn her lost childhood and adolescence. Her father had forced on her duties that were wifely chores, and she felt exploited, full of rage.

She said, as though in confirmation of my thoughts, "My father drank a lot. He also threw temper tantrums when he was displeased, when I didn't buy food he liked or he found dust on the tables. But he never hit me. Just hurled obscenities. He owned a hardware store and worked hard every day to support us. So I forgave him."

Suddenly, before my startled eyes, she broke out in hives, as her face and hands reddened. She apologized, "I feel nauseated. Like throwing up. This is what happens every time my husband makes sexual advances."

She obviously found it painful to endure intimacy. Her fear and her anger, in psychosomatic fashion, found some release through eruptions on her body rather than in words or actions. This was where Freud first started psychoanalytic theory—what he called the "conversion" of mental agony into physical symptoms—after his friend and mentor, Dr. Josef Breuer, described the success of his treatment of a young woman he called Anna O. This patient had lost drastic physical symptoms such as paralysis of a foot and acute headaches when she began to talk about memories that had terrified her. She referred to her recovery as "the talking cure." Freud credited her for starting him on the road to his monumental discoveries.

I asked Mary Winthrop, "Do you feel nervous with me?"

"Yes." A whisper.

I realized that, for her, talking to me in analysis, recalling painful memories and desires, was like having sex with her husband, in whose presence she also developed hives and felt nauseated. This was not going to be an easy patient, I thought.

As if she had read my mind, she asked nervously, "Will you take me as a patient?"

"Yes," I said. "Can you come three times a week?" This is the minimum for psychoanalysis. Five times a week is preferred but few can afford Freud's ideal schedule.

"That will be fine," she said. "My husband can afford it. He wants me to feel happier."

And probably wants a sexual partner who is not frightened to death of intimacy, I thought. (At this point I had not formulated the notion that a chronic marital complaint is an unconscious wish.)

We set up a three-day-a-week schedule. Then, looking at her watch, she rose like a wraith from the chair, slipped quietly past me, and went out the door, leaving me with my thoughts. I realized her long silences had aroused memories of my youth, when attractive young women did not want to have anything to do with me. As a result of this difficult first session with Mary I recalled the times as an adolescent when, with much trepidation, I would ask a pretty girl to dance, only to be turned down. I felt in Mary's presence, with her brief, sometimes curt responses to my questions, that I was in the company of an angry, silent virgin who warned, "Keep your distance, Buster."

I was trying to cope with my feelings of rejection yet at the same time empathize with Mary's fears. This is one of the major dilemmas of an analyst—he faces his fair share of conflicts as well as challenges. Fundamentally, the analyst responds to these conflicts like any other mortal. When he meets a woman for the first time, sees her become nauseated and break out in hives, he cannot feel pleased with himself nor, despite all the analytic literature to the contrary, can he remain "neutral." He may *behave* neutrally as he tries to empathize with her suffering, but he will experience all the emotions anyone else feels when rejected.

21

I also thought of what all my mentors in psychoanalysis had told me: ninety percent of my time would be spent listening, not saying a word. But how could I listen to a patient who did not talk? Mary had been silent during most of the first session, responding only briefly to my questions. From most patients would have flowed a stream of words and free associations about spouse or parents or friends or employers. All analysts expect their patients to talk, to say everything that comes to mind.

It takes many years, I would wager, for most analysts to genuinely accept the fact that the patient's talking to an empathic listener constitutes at least fifty percent of the cure. Because young therapists feel they have to earn their keep, they tend to talk too much. This interferes with the patient observing himself, saying what he thinks, feels, and remembers of the past.

I have found that sometimes the most therapeutic session with a patient occurs when I do not utter a single word during the forty-five minutes. For the person who has never been in analysis, it is difficult to believe that as the analyst sits in silence the patient's tensions recede. His thoughts become clearer, and he faces the ways in which he has distorted the important experiences of his life, past and present.

There is another important reason the analyst remains silent. As the patient describes his thoughts and feelings, with limited participation from the analyst, the patient starts to have feelings and fantasies about the analyst. This is what we analysts are talking about when we refer to the "transference." The patient's reactions to the analyst will be similar to his reactions to his spouse, parents, siblings, children, employers, friends, and colleagues. When the patient recognizes this similarity, he will sense how he has written his own script. He has assigned certain roles to the people to whom he feels close, much as he assigned his parents certain roles (among them the role of God, who must grant the child's every wish).

As the analyst listens, what does he think about? The analytic literature provides some answers. For one, he forms "hypotheses"—speculations about possible unconscious meanings of the patient's words and thoughts. He listens for what is *not* said, as well as what is said. He tries to figure out common themes in the patient's thoughts that match themes in his everyday life.

The analytic literature however does not describe fully the analyst's feelings, fantasies, and conflicts as he listens to the patient. I have rarely read of an analyst admitting he felt bored in a session, as occasionally happens. Or that he grew sleepy and may even have dozed off for a few seconds, as Dr. Paul Federn once confessed he did. I have fallen asleep three times in my thirty years as an analyst, each time for only five to ten seconds, and each time a dream woke me. The dream was always the same—I was making an interpretation to the patient. The dream tried to compensate for my guilt at falling asleep by carrying out my wish to produce for the patient by giving an interpretation. I found it easy to be empathic to one patient who had a regular early-morning session and would occasionally oversleep, showing up late. He sometimes reported a dream that compensated for his oversleeping; in this dream he imagined he was in my office busily free associating (carrying out his special task).

Rarely does an analyst talk about his erotic fantasies when an attractive woman on the couch tells him he is the most desirable man in the world. Though a few analysts have married their patients, most will send a patient to another analyst after realizing they have fallen in love. I find it fascinating there are few, if any, statements in the literature relating to one fantasy that many analysts have about attractive women patients—what it would be like to marry them and live with them. (Women analysts readily admit that they think this about male patients.) And, on the other side of the coin, few analysts will talk freely of their retaliatory fantasies—the ones they have when they are being disparaged, demeaned, or cursed by the patient for not being more helpful. At times they must want to say to a provocative patient, "Shut up, you ungrateful son of a bitch."

Analysts feel both pleasure and displeasure while listening to a patient. They may feel temptations of a sexual or aggressive nature, fantasies they must monitor constantly and try to understand. Frequently what an analyst feels in the session—anger, sexual passion, impotency, excitement, indifference—may be what the patient unconsciously wants the analyst to feel, but psychoanalytic relationships are not always this simple. Analysts have written that anything the analyst feels is "induced" by the patient and therefore can be interpreted by blaming the patient: "You want me to feel sexual passion," or hatred or indifference. But it must not be forgotten, and it should be stressed, that the analyst enters the relationship with pre-formed transferences, just as the patient does.

My new patient, Mary Winthrop, was ready to see me as a father who would exploit her and as a mother who had been unavailable since Mary was six. I was all ready to see her as a young date whom I wanted to dance with and seduce. When I discussed this case later with colleagues, instead of talking about my emotional reaction—a wish from adolescence to seduce young women friends—I spoke only of my wish to make Mary "comfortable" in the analytic situation so she would feel "free" to share her memories with me and benefit from the sharing.

At times I have wondered how any male analyst can remain neutral while he is alone in a room with an attractive woman lying on a couch, taking part in what Dr. Reuben Fine calls "the intimate hour." As I mentioned in the introduction I have sometimes wondered if many analysts have heart attacks and need to take long vacations frequently because they are so busy denying and repressing their own feelings in emotionally charged sessions.

Analysts constantly feel a desire either to oppose or to support the patient. At times they also feel like giving inappropriate advice, such as getting a divorce or leaving a job. Also, all analysts, whether they admit it or not, want their patients to talk. I believe that analysts feel more warmly toward those patients who speak openly about their wishes and fears, make the analysts their most important confidante, relate dreams at almost every session, practically analyze the dreams by themselves in the session, pay their bills on time, and do not offer overwhelming obstacles to treatment. These ideal patients, however, are few in number.

When a patient does not talk freely, the analyst usually asks, "What comes to mind?" or "What are your associations?" Most patients reveal what they have held back, and the analysis moves on. When a patient does not talk—analysts call this a direct form of "resistance"—the analyst will usually ask, "Are you frightened to say what you think?" implying the patient does not have to feel afraid in the analyst's presence; he will not condemn the most violent or vicious of wishes and thoughts. Most patients will soon start to report their thoughts.

Talking to an analyst has different meanings to different patients. To some, it feels like pleasurably making love. To others, it feels like confessing sins to a priest or a parent. Talking may also be a form of exhibitionism, where the patient is onstage and hopes to be applauded. Talking can also make the patient feel like a child being force-fed, or sitting on a "potty" having to "make" for an exacting parent, or having to gratify his mother and father's every request but receiving little or nothing for himself—as in Mary's instance. To some, talking can represent a rape, where the patient must psychologically undress and turn himself over to the rapist/analyst. For many patients, to talk feels demeaning—they must produce for a silent, austere authority who collects a lot of money and does very little while the patient does all the work.

Mary had great difficulty talking freely. She responded to me just as she did to her husband when he pressured her to have sex: she retreated into silence, broke out in hives, and became nauseated; she wanted only to remain passive and silent. Silence meant safety—it was the way she protected herself from her wish to explode in fury and destroy those who had hurt her as a child, and those she now saw, in displaced, distorted fashion, as wanting to hurt her.

After Mary's consultation, the sessions changed into a regular psychoanalysis. In our first meeting, she had confided in succinct form her sexual problem, marital conflict, and a few aspects of her relationship to her mother and father. But for the most part she remained silent—very, very silent—after breaking out in hives and feeling nauseated. It occurred to me that just as she resisted closeness to her husband and felt ill when he wanted intimacy, so, too, did she feel disgusted with the intimacy of the psychoanalytic scene, with the idea of sharing with me her feelings about her past and present. I had asked, toward the middle of the consultation, noticing her pained face, "Are you feeling nauseated?" She had nodded, unable to say a word, fearful she would throw up.

One of the difficult times for an analyst occurs when the patient shows deep distress, as Mary did when she broke out in hives and felt nauseated. At such an overwhelming moment the patient may not be able to talk. It has been axiomatic in psychoanalysis that if the patient can put into words his feelings, thoughts, fantasies, and memories, then bodily symptoms usually vanish. But what can an analyst do when a patient is so terrified of his feelings that he dare not verbalize them?

Here I was with Mary, who would not, could not, talk. I faced a dilemma. On the one hand, I wanted her to speak to me so she would be relieved of her distress. Yet if I pushed her to talk, no matter how gently, it would be as if her husband were pushing her into a sexual act she could not endure because it was so terrifying that to her it would be rape.

How could I show Mary I understood her pain and at the same time try to relieve it?

Sometimes I find it helpful to explain my dilemma to the patient in terms of his experience. So, at the second session, after Mary took her seat and was even more silent than during the first, I said, "I know you're suffering an enormous struggle. You resent being pushed to talk, even though a part of you knows that talking will help you."

She stared at me as if I had not said a word. We spent the rest of the hour in a silence interrupted only by my occasional anxious comments. At one point I said, "It's difficult to talk, I know." Silence. Ten minutes later I tried again: "What comes to mind?" Silence. Then I saw the hives breaking out on her face.

Each time I spoke, trying to persuade her to speak in return, she grew more and more rigid, and I saw the hives spreading. I sighed, gave up, retreated into my silence.

Sudden memories of my mother arose. I thought of how much I had wanted her love and how deprived of it I felt when she punished me by refusing to talk to me. Mary represented in many ways the mother I could never satisfy, no matter what I did. Who kept telling me she wanted nothing to do with me if I did not obey her commands to work hard for her by keeping my room clean and being a very good boy in other ways. The night before this session with Mary I had phoned my mother to ask how she was, only to hear her say nervously, "I can't speak to you now. I'm too concerned because I haven't heard from your sister since yesterday." I felt as unwanted by my mother as I did by Mary, who also did not want to talk to me. I recalled the feeling of childhood and adolescence: "I want the woman—

mother—to respond to me but 'segornisht helfun.'" This was a Yiddish expression my mother often used, meaning, "Nothing helps."

I thought how Mary's husband must have felt when she rejected him, as I now experienced myself as unwanted, impotent, pushed away in loathing. While I knew Mary wanted me to feel some of these emotions, unconsciously telling me how she felt about her husband, like all analysts I had to deal with the rejection in my unique manner, with my habitual ways of coping.

One of my major difficulties in life, on which I spent much time in my personal analysis, was dealing with rejection. Now here in my office, despite all my psychoanalytic sophistication and my awareness of Mary's conflicts, I was affected emotionally by a woman who silently told me, as my mother sometimes did, "No matter how hard you try, I will not talk to you."

Most analysts in a similar situation would describe the patient's behavior as part of Mary's transference and resistance to analysis. Mary experienced me as she did her husband when he made sexual advances she could not tolerate, and as she did her father who demanded that she "produce" around the house. In the meantime, I, like all analysts in such a situation, had to deal with what an unresponsive woman meant to me.

An unresponsive woman means different things to different men and therefore different things to different analysts. Each analyst, if he is to help an unresponsive woman patient, must become aware of his reactions to each such patient. I had to carefully review the many times I had felt like an impotent, rejected lover to my mother and to adolescent girl friends. I had to deal with the anger and hurt I had felt toward them and that I now felt with Mary. I had to keep these feelings separate from my work with her, as much as possible. This was to be an ongoing job with Mary and is an ongoing job for all analysts with every patient. The analyst

28

should ask, "Who does this patient remind me of? What emotion or wish or fantasy am I bringing to this analysis that really does not belong but is present because it is a conflictual part of my life?"

For the next several sessions, Mary found it difficult to say a word. She broke out in hives, cold sweats, felt nauseated. She told me she threw up on the street after leaving the building. I continued to feel weak, frustrated, impotent, but I also felt challenged, and because I am persistent, I would not give up. I was determined to help Mary get involved in her treatment so she could live a happier life, free from the terrifying ghosts of the past.

As I reflected on my need to persuade her to talk and produce, I realized I was dealing with a second personal problem—my own strong desire to succeed. I looked at the treatment of Mary as a course in which I needed to get an A, but which I was flunking. The idea of failure in any area of life important to me has always been repugnant. I realized I was pushing Mary to succeed in treatment and pushing myself to succeed as a therapist, the way I had been pushed as a child.

It was painful but liberating to know that by trying to persuade Mary to talk I was acting out my own ambitions, which she experienced as pressure to produce, something she had resented strongly from early childhood on. I said to myself, "Strean, you jerk, the woman's major resistance is her unwillingness to give you the time of day. She is unable to have anything to do with her husband or anybody else in an intimate sense, and you're trying to force her to do so. No wonder she's so disgusted she wants to vomit when she leaves your office."

After this insight, I could identify with Mary. I recognized the pressures of my past and present to "produce" and all the resentments I, like Mary, had felt. When an analyst can truly see in himself conflicts similar to the ones the patient currently expresses, and when he faces the fact that patient and therapist are similar, this is when we hit therapeutic awareness.

If Mary was to feel better and function better, sexually and otherwise, she needed from me what I had always longed for as a child and adolescent—someone who would convey the message, "I love you whether you produce or not." How could I do this for Mary?

Slowly, it dawned on me that if talking to me was equivalent in her mind to having sex with her husband or producing cleanliness around the house or meals for her alcoholic, demanding father, the best thing I could do was to say in effect, "It's okay if you don't talk. I will still care for you and not abandon you." I realized that Mary's early deprivation of a mother—at the age of six, when she had to become the woman of the house—was a loss she had probably never mourned. Mourning does not come easily to children—nor does it, may I add, to most adults.

This was not an easy decision because, as I have indicated, psychoanalysis gets its results through patients talking, not withholding their thoughts. I knew I was probably going against every psychoanalytic precept I had learned and violating every instruction from my teachers. But I made up my mind to follow through on this (as a golfer, I knew that the follow-through of a swing was vital to a good shot).

The next session, when Mary sat in the chair, I said, with the quiet assurance that follows the facing of a hidden truth, "It's clear to me that my trying to help you talk is making you feel worse. I think it would be best if you do not talk and we see what happens."

I added, "If at some point you want to talk, I will be ready to listen. But it might be helpful now to see how you feel if you do not talk."

Mary's hives, which had appeared when I first started to open my mouth, vanished before I had finished speaking. She looked at me, for the first time, with gratitude in those large brown eyes. She smiled wanly, as though she now felt understood. Her posture changed from a slouch to an erect position. It was clear she felt relieved, as though she'd been granted a pardon from the psychic executioner's sword.

Then, unbelievably, but true to my resolution, for the next four months, three times a week, I would greet Mary with a "Hello" or "Come in," she would nod, sit down beside the paintings of Paris streets, and we would spend forty-five minutes in mutual silence.

At the end of each month she would pay her fee, and I would say, "Thank you for the check." That was it.

Along the way, though I knew that not forcing her to talk was helpful and I could see for myself she felt more relaxed, no longer pressured, I became torn about my approach. I felt somewhat guilty. I was getting paid an ample fee for doing nothing—a violation of the work ethic that was so much a part of my life. During moments of silence, memories arose of my father castigating me for being lazy when I came in second instead of first in my class. And of my mother's constant refrain, "All play and no work makes Herbie a dumb boy." The silence with Mary made me feel as if I were playing hooky from school. I felt like a fraud, violating many ethical imperatives of my own and getting paid for my laziness.

Things got both better and worse. During the third month of this period of silence, Mary's stockbroker husband, Jonathan, phoned. He said in a deep, pleased voice, "I'm calling to express my gratitude, Dr. Strean. I don't know what you're doing with my wife, but she's a new woman. She's lost her depression. And sex is great. You're a genius."

My mouth fell open in amazement. I had not the slightest clue from her that she had changed in any way. To me, she was still the silent, maligned Mary, hiding from herself and me deep, unconscious quarries filled with fear and rage. Could silence have paid off in such high, happy returns? What was I doing that I did not know about?

Her husband followed up his first call by referring several of his friends to me for treatment. He would, from time to time, send notes expressing warm appreciation for the way his wife had changed. I felt mixed emotions. I was pleased Mary and he were enjoying intimacy at long last, and I accepted that my silent approach had somehow helped. Yet I continued to feel like a crook for being paid to sit on my rear, saying not a word.

As I do with all phone calls from patients' relatives, I asked Jonathan, explaining it would be helpful, to tell Mary he had called. I had no way of knowing whether he told her—she still was not speaking to me.

I was tempted to ask if her husband had told her of his call, but recalled the words Freud kept on his desk: "When in doubt, don't."

But then, more out of my own needs than Mary's, at the end of the fourth month, when I could no longer tolerate my guilt and what to me was a fraudulent attitude, I broke the silence.

I asked, "How do you think our work is going these last few months?"

Then she said, "You don't make me put out for you. And it's the first time in my life I've met somebody who doesn't force me to put out."

I felt reassured. She said no more, nor did I. The silence continued for another two months—six in all. She appeared on time, as always, paid at the end of each month for what I still felt was my doing nothing except being there. During the silences I often free-associated (what else was there to do?) as, over and over, I examined my quandary. On the one hand, I patted myself on the back, thought, "Strean, you're terrific. You figured out a way to help a very difficult person." On the other hand, I felt very uncomfortable doing little except to sit in silence. As I look back on the experience of saying nothing and receiving only silence, minute by minute, it was one of my most difficult hours—hours upon hours, so to speak.

Then after six months of silence, Mary's behavior shifted radically. She started to arrive late for sessions, something she had never done. I knew she was trying to tell me something important through this delinquent act. I felt at long last I had to deal with it verbally.

After she sat down one day, I said to her what I would have said to any patient under similar circumstances: "I've noticed you've been arriving late. I wonder if you feel something you can't tell me that the lateness expresses."

To my utter amazement, words now poured out of the mouth of this previously tongue-tied woman. Not just words but words of vituperative fury. In a loud, clear voice she castigated me: "You lazy bum! You sit on your ass and collect money for doing nothing. I'm thinking of reporting you to your professional organization, exposing you as the fraud you are."

Before I could open my mouth to stand up for myself, she added, "You remind me of my worthless father, who sat on his ass and did nothing while I worked my head and tail off."

I decided to say nothing. Obviously, as I had thought, her lateness was a clue to the buried anger that at long last was starting to reach a conscious level. It now bubbled like lava, from a volcano ready to explode. Up to this moment the anger had been denied because of its intensity at a very early time in her life, when she had been forced to take over her dead mother's duties, and because of her fear of defying her angry, alcoholic father. When she married, it was expressed in her hives and nausea.

Now, after our six months of sharing silences, she felt free enough with me (for the first time in her life free with someone) to dare put into words the hatred she had buried beneath layers of acquiescence. I reminded her of her powerful father and formerly feared husband. At last she could become aware of a rage long denied.

Incidentally, I called Mary "Mrs. Winthrop" for many months because it seemed clear to me that my calling her by her first name would be too frightening to her. It would be a sign of intimacy, a feeling she could not trust or tolerate. But later in treatment, when it was evident she had become involved with me in a human relationship and a psychic journey that embodied a mutual effort, to continue to call her Mrs. Winthrop would be to refer to her in a way I did not experience her. After a year of treatment she was "Mary" and I was "Herb."

I have often been asked by analytic colleagues and students the correct way to address a patient. Actually, there is no correct way, in my opinion. It depends on where analyst and patient are in terms of their relationship. Just as it would be presumptuous of me to call Mrs. Winthrop "Mary" at our first meeting, it would be equally inappropriate, I believed, to call her "Mrs. Winthrop" after I had known her a few years, had been recipient of the most intimate details of her life, and had become the most important person in her life, past and present, at times more important than her mother and father, as I helped her master the traumas of her past.

Many analysts believe that calling a patient by the first name gratifies the patient too much, as if the patient were a child, a lover, a spouse, or perhaps a friend. There is no doubt certain patients use this first-name basis to feel, "Yes, indeed, I am my analyst's child," or "lover" or "spouse." But if a patient wants to be the analyst's child, lover, or spouse, which all patients do at one point or another in treatment, this should be dealt with as an analytic issue.

The longer I have been in practice and the more comfortable I have felt with the patient's wishes and fantasies of intimacy, and the less fearful of my own responses to their wishes for closeness, I have found myself referred to more and more

often as "Herb" and less and less often as "Dr. Strean." I
have also found myself calling patients by their first names
sooner in treatment as I have grown older. I am convinced
that when analysts compulsively and rigidly refer to patients
as Mr., Mrs., or Miss, unwittingly they show they fear intimate relationships, though perhaps they would be the last
ones to acknowledge this fear. Many an analyst avoids calling
his patients anything, but this, too, avoids the issue.

When I hear patients refer to me as "Dr." and expect me
to use Mr., Mrs., or Miss over a long period of time, I consider
this a problem to be explored in the analysis. I will ask the
patient what he is frightened of if he calls me by my first
name or if I call him by his first name.

As Mary continued her verbal assaults, I felt mixed emotions. On the positive side, just hearing her talk was a
pleasure. I knew by expressing her anger she felt safer with
me and could learn to know herself better. I also knew the
expression of anger would have a curative effect as she
realized she did not have to act on it, only face it.

Yet, on the negative side, there was a part of me that
took her accusations personally, even though I told myself
they were a result of the transference: "Nothing personal
in them, Strean. Those verbal blasts are all aimed at her
daddy's head for treating her like a beast of burden." Yet I
also felt like a fraud when Mary called me a fraud. I felt
like a lazy bum when she called me a lazy bum. I felt I was
violating the work ethic when she accused me of violating
the work ethic.

For the next several sessions she continued her attacks,
and I said not a word in my defense. I told her, "I'm glad
you feel free to criticize me. This is necessary for our work."
But I felt like a bad boy with my mother, not doing my job
right. The more I could reflect on how I had often felt with
my mother and on how, once again, I was in touch with my
wish to be approved by her, the more I could see Mary as
someone quite separate from me and my past.

As we said in our book, *Guilt: Letting Go*, when someone feels uncomfortable about attacks by others, he should ask, "What do I feel guilty about that makes me take anyone's criticism so seriously?"

I realized after much thought that I had derived pleasure from Mary's doing nothing and my doing nothing. My silence with Mary was like a dream come true. Not only for Mary was our "non-working alliance" therapeutic, but for me, too. It was a joy of joys I could only vaguely appreciate while experiencing it. How often I would have liked to snarl at my mother and father, my teachers, and later my extended family, "I will *not* work. I will *not* produce for you. I hate you for pushing me."

Mary and I were rebels *with* a cause. I was enjoying going against the psychoanalytic establishment, the parental establishment, and every symbol of authority. When Mary attacked me verbally I realized my discomfort had much to do with my guilt over the pleasure of flouting authority by doing nothing. Even though my approach proved therapeutic, because my fantasies, unconscious most of the time, were ones of rebellion and hostility, I was ready to be attacked because I felt guilty.

As I slowly resolved my need for punishment and no longer had to make Mary into a punitive mother, I could move with her to the next stage of treatment. I showed her I had disappointed her the same way her parents did by seeming unavailable (a small child does not reason that a dead mother is unavailable but can only protest the unavailability). Mary welcomed the fact that I did not have to be a defensive, parental figure. She was visibly touched when I could show understanding of her wish to receive for a change, rather than always have to give—the way she felt as a child and adolescent with her father.

During her eighth month in treatment, by which time she was lying on the couch, she commented, "If you had talked earlier, it would have felt like sour milk. You would have reminded me of my sick mother."

I wondered if perhaps her mother's milk had tasted sour to Mary as a baby, and how this would have affected her feelings about her mother. Perhaps she fantasied, as all children do when a parent dies, she caused her mother's death and was unable to face her guilt. An analyst has to take literally every word a patient utters as a possible clue to the patient's feelings in connection with a long-buried trauma.

The unconscious never forgets a trauma, for part of its function is to keep the trauma repressed so the conscious can deal with everyday life. Mary could not recall the experience of tasting sour milk from her mother's breast or from a bottle her mother held while feeding her. But by recalling the sour milk in connection with her thoughts about me, she told me of a vital fact about her early childhood in relation to her lost mother—a circumstance that caused her fear, anger, and guilt.

From then on, the treatment became similar to the typical psychoanalytic journey. Mary talked freely of dreams and memories. She faced herself slowly without feeling pressured. She was able to mourn her mother's early death and her own cheerless childhood. She became more understanding of her father's alcoholism as a part of his mourning, for he began to drink heavily only after he lost his wife and faced bringing up three daughters.

Mary also had to work through her early-aroused sexual, oedipal passion for her father as she took her mother's place in all respects but the sexual. Her forbidden desire for her father, natural to every little girl so she can later transfer this desire to a more appropriate man, was more intense than that of the average daughter. Mary lacked a mother as the rival who would be a brake on her passions. All feeling for her father would have to be deadened, as it was for her husband, until she entered treatment, faced her hidden fear and fury, and could mourn the devastating loss of her mother at so early an age.

With her new awarenesses, Mary experienced her marriage as more pleasurable. After she left analysis, she went to college, majored in political science, which she had wanted to do but did not dare. Five years later, she wrote to tell me she had given birth to a son and planned to become a professor in political science at a city college within two years.

She ended the letter, "I thank you more than I can put into words for your superb help at a time in my life when I was at the crossroads."

Mary sought help early in my professional career. I was a student analyst, which meant I was supervised in my cases. I was also going through an extensive personal analysis and taking classes in psychoanalytic theory at the National Psychological Association for Psychoanalysis. One supervisor had said, as I told him of the four months of silence with Mary, "You should triple your fee with this woman. You're doing everything that does not come naturally."

This was a time when I felt in doubt about many professional tenets. I have often asked myself if I would act the same way today with Mary. I am not sure. But I believe I helped her by doing what I thought best at that moment in my analytic career.

2

WHY WON'T YOU TELL ME?
The Man Who Refused
to Give His Name

He looked as if he didn't care about his appearance or what the world thought of him. He had informed me over the phone he was thirty-two years old, worked in an advertising agency, was married. He would not give his name but said he would appear any time I was free for a consultation.

At the hour set, a man almost six feet tall, balding, over-weight, looking pale, appeared in my office. His suit, though well tailored, looked as if it had seen better-pressed days. His light brown eyes, keen, appraising, gave my consultation room the once-over before he sat down. He seemed very uncomfortable.

I had to strain to hear him, so low his voice. There was a kind of permanent sadness about his face, I thought. He did not smile; I sensed a depressed air.

A cardinal rule of psychoanalytic treatment is that the patient says whatever comes to mind. This rule is so well known that even neophytes do not need to be told about it. Often a naive, unsophisticated man or woman will lie down on the couch during the first session and say, "I know I'm supposed to tell you what I'm thinking."

I asked this man, "May I have your name?"

He looked at me, then said stubbornly, "I cannot tell you my name."

I was startled. "Oh?"

"Which means I can't pay you by check. I'll pay cash," he stated. "Put me down as Mr. X."

I was astounded—this was something new under the psychoanalytic sun—but I decided for the moment to accept his decision. "How did you happen to call me?"

"I was given your name by one of your colleagues after I called your analytic society. I wouldn't tell him my name either."

I recalled that the colleague had phoned to inform me he had referred a man who refused to give his name. Now I wondered what this patient's reason could be. Was he an escaped convict? Was he wanted for murder or grand larceny? Perhaps when he felt more at home in my office he would reveal his name.

"May I ask why you want therapy?" I asked, somewhat meekly.

"I got fired from my job as a writer of advertising copy. I'd worked at that agency for nine years. They said they had to cut costs, that I was one of five let go. I've been so depressed for weeks I can't get up enough courage to look for another job."

I waited for him to go on, glad he could at least talk fluently about his troubles.

He continued, "I'm plagued by insomnia. I suffer from peptic ulcers. I have phobias. I can't go into men's rooms at hotels or railroad stations or airports. I avoid them like the plague."

He hesitated, then admitted, "Sex isn't going well either. I don't have sex with my wife. After eight years of marriage, she doesn't interest me anymore." Then grimly: "I suppose I've never felt really free with her. She's ten years younger than I am and earns more money as a fashion designer than I did as a copywriter. I've always felt she doesn't think I'm macho enough for her."

As he sank into silence I asked, "Do you have children?"

"A daughter three years old and a son born a year ago. I try to love them, but they seem like strangers most of the time. A nurse takes care of them."

He told me more about his life. "I was always a top student, but after I graduated from the University of Chicago, where I majored in English literature, I found myself in low-paying writing jobs that brought little satisfaction."

Then he admitted, eyes fastened on my Mother and Child marble sculpture, "Most of my life I've been a loner. I was six years older than my sister. My father was a hard worker who owned a rather large department store on the north side of Chicago. He paid little attention to his children except to pressure us to study hard, and criticize us when he didn't approve of something we did. I wanted to be a writer, but he said writing was a risky way of earning a living. He died when I was seventeen, and I must say I didn't grieve much. I thought, 'That's one less burden I have to bear.'"

Again silence. Then: "My mother was both a seductive and punishing woman. I never knew whether she would embrace me or criticize me. I know she loved my sister much more. *She* got all the attention." This sounded quite familiar to me.

He laughed ironically. "I borrowed money from my wife to start therapy and to tide me over until I can find a job." He added, "I'll pay her back." Then, worriedly: "Will you take me on that basis?"

The colleague who had referred him told me he would

require four sessions a week, and at that time I needed just such a patient in order to complete my requirements so I could graduate from the analytic institute.

I asked, "Would you like to start analysis at four sessions a week and see how it goes?"

He half smiled, as though for the first time since he entered he felt somewhat pleased. "That would be fine."

As he stood up to leave, he warned, "I won't be able to stay in treatment if you insist I give you my name."

"You seem concerned that I will insist on knowing your name," I observed.

Throughout the interview he had appeared at times deferential and compliant, but always with that underlying depression. Now irritation and some defiance entered his voice. "The government frequently checks up on people," he said, "and if they find out I'm in psychoanalysis I'll never get a job." Then, almost a whine: "Are you going to *insist* on knowing my name?"

I pointed out gently, "You have used the word 'insist' at least twice. You seem concerned about how insistent I am or will be."

"I'm told psychoanalysts are very insistent people. I'm wary of them."

I suggested, "You might want another session so we can discuss further your doubts about me and psychoanalytic treatment before you make definite plans."

I do not know to this day if he was aware of my eerie, uncomfortable feeling when he told me he would not give his name, rationalizing he might then be in trouble with the government. On the one hand, I could tell myself that this was a paranoid man who saw me as a potential persecutor. On the other hand, he sounded eminently reasonable and intelligent. During my years of practice I have met certain types of paranoid men and women who seem logical as they collect injustices and talk of real or imagined enemies. To me, Mr. X, as I would call him, sounded in the first interview both like a reasonable man who wanted to protect himself and like a paranoid patient who felt he was being persecuted.

After this first interview I thought of Mr. X many times before his next appointment. I felt mildly paranoid myself. Who *was* he? Should I be suspicious of him? Uncharacteristically, I found myself mentioning the case to several colleagues. I felt challenged and rather like a detective setting out to unravel a mystery. I also felt like an adolescent again, as if I had asked a girl to give me her phone number and she had refused. But all this only spurred me on.

Mr. X started the second session by saying, "I'm glad you didn't insist on knowing my name. I'll stick with you for a while."

I was silent.

"But I'm worried that you will insist I use the couch." He stared at it as though it held a ghost.

Then he said, "I have a bad back. It's causing me acute pain this very minute. I *have* to sit upright or I'm in agony. No couch for me."

His thoughts enabled me to offer an interpretation: "You are worried I will dominate and control you by insisting you give your name and also by insisting you lie on the couch."

The interpretation was helpful and timely, for he soon told me, "My back feels better. I think we can work something out. You don't sound too insistent."

I had arrived at my interpretation by exploring my feelings when he refused to give his name and then refused to lie on the couch. I felt dominated by him, weakened by him, excluded by him. I recalled that he had told me how distant he felt from everyone in his life, and it did not surprise me that he would try to distance himself from me early in our relationship. I learned from him a lesson that I later used frequently in my work with other patients: he was doing unto me what he was afraid I would do unto him. He was behaving like a childhood bully, issuing commands because he was afraid I would dominate him as his father had. Very often, as was true here, by examining how I felt dominated and then anxious, I could eventually help a patient understand how he felt.

Most patients realize that they can gain a better understanding of the past if they face the truth about their fantasies, dreams, and thoughts—particularly their thoughts and feelings about the analyst, which reflect their childhood thoughts and feelings about their mothers and fathers. Yet every patient who has ever been in analysis resists facing this kind of truth. So embarrassing, so anxiety-provoking, so frightening are our concealed wishes and fantasies that Freud, early in the development of psychoanalysis, pointed out that if people could be honest with themselves about what they fantasied and wished for, they would not be neurotic.

The patient's constant withholding of information is a phenomenon that confronts every practicing analyst in virtually every session with every patient. This is why psychoanalytic treatment takes so long. People are seriously affected by their phobias, psychosomatic symptoms, and unhappiness in relationships, but they are often unwilling to face the truth about themselves.

It is far easier for an alcoholic to keep drinking than to acknowledge his wish to be a baby sucking at his mother's breast. It is much easier for a woman to constantly demean her husband, find fault with him night and day, than to acknowledge her wish to keep him weak and impotent.

It took me a long time to fully appreciate that all patients most of the time want to sabotage their analysis. It seemed to me for many years that if patients wanted to feel better, they would act in ways that would enhance recovery instead of blocking it.

It was only through my long personal analysis and many years of supervision and study that I could emotionally and intellectually accept the fact that just as children find it difficult to grow up, to be weaned, to be toilet trained, to take no for an answer, patients in treatment find it difficult to face the child in themselves. They fear exposing their primitive urges and fantasies more than they fear remaining crippled by them. All patients participate actively and passively, overtly and covertly, in what Freud called "resistance." Yet how analysts feel when their patients "resist" has been scarcely discussed.

The analyst's response to resistance is probably kept secret for the same reason the patient keeps secrets from the analyst. Most men and women who become analysts are intellectually curious; otherwise they would not spend so many hours each day listening to the intimate details of their patients' past and present lives—especially the sexual and violent aspects. I would suggest if an analyst is to do well in his work he has to accept that he is something of a voyeur, and he has to enjoy his voyeurism. If he does not, he is apt to be bored with his work and/or frightened much of the time by his own sexual and aggressive fantasies.

It is not easy for analysts to admit that when their voyeurism is frustrated they may become irritated. It is easier to "interpret" to the patient—to point out that he is withholding material when, instead of receiving an outpouring that rivals *Lady Chatterley's Lover*, the analyst hears only a detailed report of what the patient has done that day at work and how much he hates some of the people at the office. Perhaps an analyst will even point out somewhat reprovingly to the patient that he withholds the more important material, such as memories of his repressed feelings about his parents as he grew up.

When I researched the literature for my book, *Resolving Resistances in Psychotherapy*, I was both amused and concerned with how different analysts used the term "resistance." Over and over I found that when the patient did something that went against what the analyst wanted, this was called resistance. Very often it is difficult for an analyst to fully empathize with the fact that when a patient does not want to express facts or feelings, it means he feels afraid, or is in pain and is trying to ward off anxiety, hurt, and danger. Just as an eager lover may become upset when his partner says, "I don't want to respond to your overtures," many analysts feel upset when the patient says, overtly or covertly, "I don't want to respond to you" (get psychologically undressed in front of you). At least the lovers' disrobing is mutual, which makes it easier for both. And just as the eager lover cannot easily reassure himself, "My partner feels discomfort, anxiety and danger when I ask him to disrobe," it is often difficult for an analyst to empathize with the resistance of a reluctant patient to psychologically "disrobe."

When I was working on my book about resistance, I found it interesting that there was no psychoanalytic textbook on the subject, even though resistance is considered a universal phenomenon. I thought perhaps one reason was that a patient's many attempts to sabotage the analyst (to "pulverize" him, as Dr. Harry Stack Sullivan once put it), to fight psychic progress, to remain emotionally conflicted, are so irritating, frustrating, and depressing to analysts that they would rather not talk of it or write openly about it.

One of the things that probably helped me resolve some of my difficulties in coping with patients' resistance was that my analyst, Reuben Fine, early in my analysis, told me every patient has secrets he wants to keep from conscious memory and from his analyst as long as possible. When I, as a patient, eventually began to feel it was no great crime to resist, I became more compassionate with my patients' wishes to keep secrets from me.

Yet despite more than three decades as an analyst, I still find it difficult to relax fully when the patient, in one way or another, says, "I don't want to tell you." At such times I have felt teased, taunted, or demeaned.

Which is how I felt with the man who would not tell me his name and who refused to lie down on the couch. Yet I wanted to help him overcome his resistance against revealing his name. So the psychic sleuth in me set out to find what terrors in his life had so overwhelmed him that the very mention of his name put him in danger. He would furnish me with the clues, of that I had no doubt, in the sessions ahead.

In contrast to most patients, who will lie down on the couch, albeit somewhat reluctantly, after a few weeks, Mr. X needed to sit up for three months. To him, lying down seemed like submitting to me, becoming my "slave." I had to respect his wish to sit up and look at me.

When a patient sits opposite me, I feel somewhat self-conscious, less secure, more under the patient's scrutiny. I find myself working harder, talking more than I should, and often hoping the patient will soon choose to lie down so that I can relax.

The couch enables the patient to concentrate more fully on his thoughts without external stimuli, to more easily regress so that childhood memories will simmer to the surface and transference reactions will be more likely to occur. But the couch also protects the analyst. Freud admitted he could not stand to have men and women looking at him all day. The couch served as protection for him and helped the patient as well.

Many times I have thought of Freud's honest admission, and I remembered it often while I was working with Mr. X, who for three months glared at me accusingly. He aroused in me feelings of defensiveness. I felt he was constantly looking me over, and this stirred memories of my relationship with my father. I thought of the many times my father had berated me for being less than adequate. As Mr X kept questioning my credentials, wondering out loud if I was capable of helping him, and in other ways trying to demean me, I felt like a defenseless boy admonished by his austere, authoritarian father.

Fortunately, what analysts call my "countertransference" reaction was helpful to Mr. X, because though he criticized me, I did not retaliate. When he berated me he felt superior, stronger, and I knew he would need this added strength to reach the point where he could lie on the couch and, I hoped, give me his name—admit he had a sense of his own identity. I knew some powerful, terrifying fantasies and wishes were at work, holding him back from offering the very name that kept him distant from me. After all, our names give us our identity and he wanted to hide his from me.

In the meantime his put-downs continued. At one point he said challengingly, "You look like you were a depressed child. Did you go into psychoanalysis after being brutalized in a mental hospital?"

Another time he sneered, "When I look at you, I'm convinced you're impotent, maybe even a fairy."

I knew he was telling me something important about himself. This is what we call "projection"—hurling at someone else the very charge you are most afraid of within yourself. *He* felt like a depressed child, *he* worried about being brutalized in a mental hospital, *he* felt impotent, *he* feared he was homosexual.

But because I felt in many ways like a defenseless boy, I knew he would begin to feel more comfortable in my presence. As a matter of fact, while I listened to his accusations, hurled more speedily than Dwight Gooden's ninety-seven-mile-an-hour fastball, I recalled the statement of a former supervisor, Dr. Oscar Sternbach, an analyst from Vienna. He told me, "Don't be eager to show your patients how much you know and how strong you are. Maybe for the first time in his life a patient can reassure himself, 'I've found somebody who is more stupid and less adequate than I am.'"

As I reflected further on my thoughts about Mr. X's demeaning accusations, I realized that just as I had attempted to placate my father when he was critical of or angry at me, I now felt a wish to submit to my vitriolic patient. Again this attitude, though defensive, helped my patient. Had I emerged as defiant or self-confident, I probably would have driven him away.

We analysts often do not take into sufficient consideration how our anxieties can help or hinder psychoanalytic progress. It is quite conceivable that if I were to see a patient like Mr. X today, my air of self-confidence might force him to flee. I took him on when I was younger and less secure, however, allowing him to feel superior, as he had never felt with his father, and I was able to keep him in treatment.

Another dimension to my countertransference response to Mr. X helped me in working with him. My father, who held a Ph.D. in science, was severely critical of me much of the time. But sometimes, after days of not speaking to me or hours of reprimanding me, he would suddenly smile as if to say, "Let's not take our mutual hatred all that seriously." With Mr. X, despite all his anger and criticism, and despite my discomfort, I felt that there existed a muffled, mutual love that seemed to carry our work forward—what some analysts refer to as "the holding environment" set by the analyst.

Just as patients can feel hopeful about their future treatment when they relate to the analyst as if he were a loving figure from the past, analysts can feel hopeful about helping the patient when they relate to the patient as a loving figure from their own past. And just as a patient's transference reaction can be based on fantasies, an analyst's hope for the success of the analysis can also be based on fantasies. Dr. Karl Menninger has said that without such hope on the part of the analyst, no patient can succeed in analysis. I would add that without hope, no analyst is able to convey the feeling to the patient that he can resolve his resistances and face the truth of his life. Sometimes the hope of the analyst is too unrealistic, and sometimes the patient's hope is, too. But hope we must.

One day as I sat facing Mr. X, he spoke of his insecurity at work. He said, "I often see an employer the way I see you—as someone who insists on dominating and controlling me."

I could identify with him, having often seen my own bosses as the dominating father of my past. I empathized with how weak Mr. X felt in such a situation, just as I had felt weak with parental figures who pressured me. It was quite easy for me to say to him, "The bosses are reminiscent of your dominating father." While this interpretation came directly from my own past, it was also an accurate and understanding statement of my patient's plight.

Two weeks after the interpretation, Mr. X announced he had found work at another advertising agency and had been given more responsibility than he'd had previously. As he told me this, I saw his handsome mouth curve into a full smile for the first time since we met.

Yet, after working two weeks, he reported, "Once more I'm involved in arguments and power struggles with my boss."

He could not recognize that these conflicts emerged from within himself, that they were not being imposed on him, since the identical situation had occurred with his father and with me, but he still felt helpless in the presence of his new boss.

At this point I suggested, marking three months of treatment, "You might want to consider using the couch so you can understand better what unconsciously contributes to your problems with bosses and to your other conflicts." This was near the end of the session.

At the next session, without saying a word, he entered the room, strode directly to the couch. He lowered all six feet onto the couch slowly, reluctantly, and sighed as his head touched the pillow. Then, not content to give in so easily to my request, he charged, "You prefer me on the couch so you can be in a one-upmanship position. You can see me but I can't see you."

Then he added vindictively, "I'm glad I haven't given you my name. I'm more convinced than ever you would run to government agents and get paid for turning me in."

His hostile, accusatory, paranoid fantasies consumed the analysis for the next two months. He vehemently called me an opportunist, a manipulator, a sadist, and "probably a homosexual." I realized once again how much these projections told me about him and of how he felt about his father.

In the sixth month of treatment he described a dream. In a voice that at times sounded boyish, he said, "Last night I dreamed you screamed at me for not paying you enough and not being more productive in analysis. You insisted I tell you more fantasies, more dreams, and give more free associations."

I replied, "You feel I want you to be my slave, much as you felt you were a slave to your father."

"I guess that's true," he said grudgingly. His first admission that an interpretation might be valid.

Then he added defensively, "I'm still convinced you're involved in psychoanalytic work so you can be a slave-master and torment your patients sadistically."

A common charge by patients, I thought. As I worked with him and became the target of many more accusations, I wondered why suddenly his sadism no longer upset me. In fact, I even enjoyed it. The answer was not too difficult to find: Mr. X was criticizing me the way I wished I could have criticized my father. Just as Mr. X felt better because he struck out at me, I felt better identifying with him. I was verbally punching my father as Mr. X verbally punched me.

For many years I had wondered why I was so successful in treating juvenile delinquents and other rebellious, seemingly irredeemable antisocial youngsters. As I worked with

Mr. X, the reason became clearer. I was Mr. X in many ways, just as I was the delinquent and antisocial youngsters I treated in child guidance clinics and therapeutic camps. As these patients attacked me, I was attacking my father and other father figures I felt pressured by. This awareness in itself would never have made me a good analyst, though, for to go on hating never cured a soul. It took many years of personal analysis for me to relinquish my battle with father figures and to see myself as an adult rather than a David facing a Goliath without a slingshot.

But to this day I empathize with anyone who suffers unresolved anger toward authorities. I feel easy and comfortable when patients use me as a target for the slings and arrows of outrageous childhoods. One of my most effective acts as a father occurred when my two sons competed with one another. I asked them to form a team to oppose me in touch football. They had to cooperate with each other to defeat me—which I enjoyed.

After seven months of treatment, Mr. X assumed an interesting stance in the analysis. In many ways he became the analyst, made me the patient. He "interpreted" my motives in becoming a tormenting slave-master. He said, "You are basically a homosexual who acts tough to cover up your vulnerability" (the way he saw his father and himself).

In the eighth month of therapy he told me, "You're essentially a passive man who wants to be fucked up the ass but are too scared to admit it."

"What do you think frightens me about acknowledging my homosexuality?" I asked, wanting him to tell me what frightened him.

"You like to tease and fool the world. Maybe if you tease somebody long enough, he'll rape you in anger. That's what you really want."

I had my answer. His fantasy was that if he teased me long enough, I would rape him in anger—his reaction as a child to his teasing father, his model of what it meant to be a "man."

As he felt more relaxed with me he did not defend so much against his homosexual feelings, and as he spoke more freely of them he found he could enjoy sex with his wife. He confessed one day, "I'm sexually potent once again with my wife. She's very happy about it." (Because he was not using so much energy defending himself, he could be more relaxed in bed and elsewhere.) Then he added, "I also seem to be getting along better with my boss."

And a third achievement: "I'm enjoying my children more. Spent much of the weekend with them, which I never did before."

He managed, however, to get in his usual charges against me: "You must envy me. You are obviously celibate. You have a homosexual problem while I'm enjoying sexual pleasure with a woman."

But he was able to say, showing new insight, "I empathize with your envy of my sexual life, Dr. Strean, because I remember feeling that way about my mother and father's sexual relationship. And just as you envy my success on the job, I can remember when I was a boy and envied my father's popularity with men and his business acumen."

For several sessions he kept mocking and denigrating me (as, I judged, his father had done to him, and perhaps also as his mother had done to his father). In one dream he saw me as a pig, wearing glasses, trying in vain to work, emerging a failure. In another dream I was catcher on a homosexual baseball team.

"Why a catcher?" I asked.

"You want to sniff the batters' asses and touch their genitals while nobody is looking," he said.

While it was evident he was projecting his wishes onto me, I continued to accept being the recipient of his projections. I was reminded of the time I had purposely helped young boys in therapy beat me at checkers, identifying with them as they felt superior. Which was, of course, how I had so often wanted to feel as a boy with my father. Perhaps one of my deepest wishes as a child was to angrily hurl at my father the words, "You faggot, you fairy," just as Mr. X now hurled them at me.

In my work with him I had to monitor the gratification I received in identifying with his sadism. To let the sadism continue without modification would have left him an angry man, incapable of mature love, unable to cooperate with others. Fortunately, as he projected his homosexual wishes onto me and saw I did not react defensively or argumentatively, he slowly began to identify with my objectivity. He started at last to consider his own homosexual fantasies.

He admitted one day, "When I was a sophomore in high school and showered after gym, I found myself furtively looking at the penises of other boys."

"What were your fantasies?" I asked.

"I wanted to get close to them in the shower and suck their penises. Or screw them up the ass, or be screwed." He sounded embarrassed as he was able to admit wishes he previously thought unacceptable.

He went on, "Ever since then, I've kept these wishes secret from the world. I've been unable to urinate or defecate in public toilets because I feel so frightened of what I might do."

Now it became clear what had caused his phobia about men's rooms—the fear he would give in to his strong homosexual desires. He began to talk of homosexual fantasies with less terror, imagined them in his relationship with me. He reported dreams in which I insisted on having anal intercourse with him. He started to consider the possibility he wanted me to rape him.

He said one day, "I heard a joke. A man says to a woman, 'So help me, I'll rape you,' and the woman replies, 'So rape me; I'll help you.'" He was saying he wished I would rape him and he would be happy to help me do so.

We discussed his identification with the woman (his mother) in that joke. Though he was becoming freer in expressing his homosexual fantasies, in which he became the woman, I sensed he had never had any overt homosexual experiences. Many men, both in and out of analysis, feel that if they have homosexual fantasies they must be homosexuals. I have found, and so have other analysts, that heterosexual men—though they feel embarrassed, frightened, and anxious when they reveal homosexual fantasies—emerge differently in the analytic situation than do overt homosexuals. The latter rarely feel free to discuss their homosexual fantasies because, for them, in contrast to the heterosexuals, talking about homosexual fantasies is similar to having sex with the analyst and registers in their minds as incest, something to be shunned. Women analysts report a similar finding with women patients: heterosexual women talk more freely about homosexual fantasies than do homosexual women.

I believe that most men in our society find it difficult to face and discuss homosexual fantasies. Despite reassurances from analysts that everyone has certain homosexual feelings, men, particularly in our culture, work overtime to ward off homosexual fantasies and to repress the desire to be a woman.

One reason so many men want to appear "macho" is to deny their wish to be a woman and their fear of being feminine. It is also believed the incidence of heart attacks and psychosomatic illnesses is higher among men because they work so hard to ward off their desire to be a woman by constantly proving their masculinity. After all, the mother is in charge of the lives of most little boys during the early years when their impressions are solidly formed. They envy her because she is in the power position, emotionally speaking. The woman is the one the little boy first fears, the one who gives orders, distinguishes "right" from "wrong."

In all my years of analytic practice I have never completed a successful analysis without working for some time on a patient's wish to be a member of the opposite sex. The grass is always greener on the other sex's side. Every woman to some degree wants to be a man, envies men. Every man to some degree wants to be a woman, envies women. And yet, as Dr. Theodor Reik once said, "Because the resistance of a man to talk about his homosexuality is so strong, few men come to terms with it even when they are with good analysts."

An important factor never discussed in the psychoanalytic literature, as far as I know, is how comfortable the analyst is with his own homosexual wishes, his fantasies about being a member of the opposite sex. I have felt quite comfortable in helping men resolve their resistances to discussing homosexuality because I spent a long time in my personal analysis facing this resistance. Because I feared my strong competitive drives toward my father, who seemed during much of my childhood and adolescence to be Mr. Perfection—brilliant, athletic, and inventive—I unconsciously frequently behaved with him like a submissive wife or lovable daughter.

As I worked with Mr. X, I recalled my own initial strong reluctance to face my envy of women and, later, my strong conviction that girls and women have it much better than men. I thought about Mr. X's great fear of being—and strong wish to be—a girl or woman. I recalled how much I envied my beautiful sister, who was praised for getting C's while I had to get A's to receive praise. I recalled my jealousy of my mother, who only had to look attractive to make my father smile, while I had to hit home runs and be first in my class in order to receive a less loving smile. As I empathized with Mr. X, I remembered the many times I was convinced that my own analyst preferred his women patients to me. I felt sure if I were a woman he would offer me more "penetrating" interpretations and other "interventions" that would touch me more deeply.

I had been fortunate in having the opportunity to face the woman in myself during my personal analysis, to spend time analyzing the part of me that wanted to be like my mother, my sister, and other women. This not only helped me understand my men patients but also allowed me to identify with women patients and their wishes and fantasies.

One time I asked Dr. Paul Federn, "Why have you been so successful in analyzing women patients?"

Dr. Federn, a tall, bearded, virile man, who emerged in my mind as extremely masculine, casually responded, "Because I like the woman in me."

I have often reminded myself of this answer and have from time to time mentioned it to some of my male patients and students. They usually use the remark to their therapeutic advantage.

After a year and a half Mr. X described a dream in which I raped him unmercifully. As he told me about the dream, he was obviously anxious and embarrassed about wishing I would sadistically rape him. But then he started to laugh. When his laughter subsided, I asked, "What were you thinking about when you laughed?"

He said, a note of triumph in his voice, "You entered my vagina." Then, in explanation: "My name sounds like 'vagina.' At least my name has 'Regina' in it. It's Reginald, a sissy name. Reginald Sheffield." He added, "My friends call me Reggie."

His name was finally out of the bag, so to speak. Reginald—Regina—Vagina. The part for the whole, the way the unconscious often speaks. Sometimes even one letter, such as an initial, offers the clue.

Sounding relieved, he went on, "I enjoyed teasing you all these months by refusing to tell you my name, but I think enough is enough." He was saying he finally trusted me. I had shown him I would never tease him, as his father had done, to humiliate him. To tease someone is to verbally attack him.

I felt quite elated. As I analyzed my feelings of elation it became clear my reaction was like a sexual triumph wherein, as in Reginald's dream, I was like a seducer—a teasing, sadistic, prospective lover. The dream had led to his telling me his name, a victory for me as well as for him.

I was uncomfortable about my jubilation until I realized I was feeling discomfort over a homosexual fantasy. I did not want to admit it could be fun to seduce an indifferent man. But in a boyish way, it was. As though I were able to seduce my indifferent father, change his feelings toward me from indifference to love.

I also felt triumph in finally knowing who Mr. X was. No longer was he partly unreal, to himself or to me. He was ready to assume his own identity, which meant the analysis was progressing.

Times like this are difficult for an analyst. If he is honest with himself, not too inhibited, he is bound to show what pleases him in the analysis. Yet he also knows if the patient becomes too sensitive to what pleases and displeases the analyst, this can interfere with the patient's ability to talk freely, to truly reveal himself.

When the analyst's predilections become apparent, a compliant patient becomes overcompliant and an oppositional patient overly oppositional. Therefore, it is good analytic technique not to impose one's pleasures and biases onto the analytic work. But sometimes it becomes apparent to the patient that the analyst is pleased or displeased, and the patient becomes attuned to how the analyst feels. I have found it more helpful to the patient to ask what he feels about my pleasure or displeasure than to deny the way I feel or the way the patient thinks I feel.

During the next session Reginald Sheffield told me I seemed more relaxed and relieved, now that I knew his name. I did not deny his perception but asked how he felt about my less tense appearance. He said, "I think you've been working too hard and need a rest" (how he felt about himself).

I agreed silently. He had been a difficult patient. No analyst likes to be criticized and condemned for months on end.

He went on, "I had a dream in which I was a teacher discussing with my students the derivation of the word 'secret.'"

As he told me his thoughts about the dream he made his own interpretation: "There is a similarity between the word 'secret' and the word 'secretion,' and the dream is my way of making two more confessions to you—two more 'secrets.' The first one is that I masturbate two or three times a day, have for years. I enjoy 'secreting' a lot of sperm."

"Why did you feel you had to hold back this information?" I asked.

"Because as I masturbate I have the fantasy of raping a man or being raped by a man. This was too shameful and embarrassing to talk about."

His often-expressed accusation that I wanted to rape him thus represented his own wish to rape me or to be raped by me, and this he could now admit to himself.

He added, "When I started to imagine that I raped you or was being raped by you, sucking you and being sucked off by you, I thought it was time to talk about it in analysis."

Reginald acknowledged that while his guilt, shame, and embarrassment had made him refrain from analyzing his compulsive masturbation, his holding back information from me had also made him feel powerful; it was a way of teasing me. He could tease me in the way he had been teased by his parents who, he said, "both walked around in the nude while I was growing up but never gave me very much emotionally, always held back on me."

Parents who appear nude in front of children may stimulate the children sexually. His parents had done this to him, teasing, never gratifying. He had repeated this "teasing" with me in the analysis.

Then he revealed his second "secret." He said, "I never told you I was a top student in college, then started to fail when the possibility of earning a degree became a reality. I feared you would be envious of me and reject me as a patient if I shared my academic excellence with you."

He believed I would not help him if I knew he had been an outstanding student, just as he thought his achievements in college would activate envy and rage in his father and thus had to be avoided—again a projection of the envy and rage he felt toward his openly seductive father. Often the homosexual man has a seductive father, although the psychoanalytic literature has stressed primarily the seductive mother.

As Reginald revealed his carefully guarded secrets, I found myself feeling very compassionate, identifying with him. While he confessed his compulsive masturbation, I recalled the many times in my own analysis when I would take a deep breath and admit either a shameful fantasy or something I had done in reality about which I felt guilty. I knew that what helped me resolve my embarrassment and reduce my guilt was my analyst's nonjudgmental, understanding attitude. This I could now show with Reginald.

When he told me of his embarrassment and inhibition about academic success, I felt I was looking in the mirror. I had spent many years in my analysis talking about not being able to enjoy my achievements because I often used them as a way of competing against my father, my uncle, or one of several other father figures, including my analyst. Most people, I realized, fail to enjoy their achievements or are inhibited from achieving because they have not faced their wish to murder competitive figures in childhood. People either prevent themselves from achieving or punish themselves for having achieved.

As Reginald's analysis neared its end, he gained further understanding of why he had to keep his intellectual capacities and achievements "secret." To succeed academically or on the job was an oedipal victory that made him feel guilty for "being too murderous and too sexual." He pointed out that at age fourteen, when he was having incestuous fantasies about his mother and sister as well as angry and murderous fantasies about his father, his father suddenly died. I realized Reginald felt he had killed his father.

A dream during the last phase of analysis confirmed this. It revealed what Reginald called his "biggest, deepest, and worst secret." He walked in one morning, lay down on the couch, said slowly and reluctantly, "Last night I dreamed my mother and my sister were putting on their bathrobes over their nude bodies while my father lay dying on the floor in front of them. I was there, too, and as I looked at my dead father I felt not sorrow but glee that he was dead. I woke up feeling very guilty and ashamed of how I felt." He went on, "I felt somehow I had killed my father and taken over my mother and sister. I was the victorious murderer."

As he was able to get in touch with his profound guilt over the wish to kill his father and "take over" (sexually) his mother and sister, he felt more comfortable with his bosses, whose job he unconsciously wanted to "take over." He also said he was afraid to become my "equal," which led him to reveal another secret, one far less unconscious. His dreams and fantasies showed he believed if he succeeded on the job and in life it would mean he had succeeded in analysis. "This would give you too much satisfaction; I don't want you to feel too smug," he teased, but not in jest.

His last months of analysis consisted primarily of examining the secret pleasure he derived from defeating me by not accepting my interpretations. As he became more aware of his strong oedipal wishes to defeat me and his deep homosexual yearning to hold on to me as a benign father figure, he was able to end the analysis, move on to a happier home life and a burgeoning career.

His secretiveness, teasing, and preoccupation with sexual fantasies had kept me on my psychic toes. He enjoyed teasing me because he received sadistic gratification from what he believed to be my torment rather than facing his own painful suffering. In me he had found a parental figure who gave him full attention, did not degrade him, listened to his every word with respect, wanted him to give up his suffering.

Like most patients who keep secrets from their analysts, he projected his critical conscience onto me, feared my anger and disapproval. In teasing me, he could move from his childhood position of victim to that of victor, from passive child to powerful director, experiencing a sense of mastery rather than feeling castrated, humiliated.

One of his most important motives in keeping his name secret was his unconscious wish to be raped by me (his childhood wish, as he saw his father seductively walk naked in front of him so many times). This wish was tied to his fear of telling his name, which contained in it reference to the wish to be the defenseless woman his father raped. When he could face this wish, as well as the wish to be raped by his father, he could tell me his name.

His comments about the similarity between the words "secret" and "secretion" were quite perceptive. They parallel the ideas of writer and psychoanalyst Marie Bonaparte, who said that confessing a secret was like confessing masturbation.

Reginald's secret murderous wishes, coupled with his incestuous wishes, explained his wish to keep secret his academic accomplishments and intellectual potential. Doing well academically and professionally was unconsciously equated with destroying his father and seducing his mother— his "biggest, deepest, and worst secret."

Finally, he had to keep his negative therapeutic reaction a secret. He could not successfully end treatment until he became aware of his secret wish to defeat me, deprive me of the gratification of helping him.

I found dealing with Reginald's oedipal difficulties like old home week. One of the most difficult times in my life occurred when my father went to Israel in 1947 during the Israeli-Arab war. I stayed at home with my mother and sister, and we all wondered if my father would return home. Like Reginald, I felt smug and triumphant in taking over my father's position as head of the household, but I also felt intense guilt about wishing he would die so that I would have my mother and sister all to myself. These fantasies and memories were revived during my work with Reginald. Because, thanks to my analysis, I no longer felt guilty about them, I was able to empathize with Reginald.

My work with him was not particularly difficult, because he reminded me of parts of myself I had shared with my analyst, but there were a few times, especially in the early phases, when I felt irritated, resented being teased by him. From time to time I fantasied I would insist he tell me his name, thus complying with his fantasy to be forced into submission—raped. As I analyzed my wish that he reveal his name, I realized I had been turning him into the powerful father who dominated me and whom I had wanted to put down.

Had I given in to this fantasy, Reginald would undoubtedly have felt threatened, left treatment. In contrast to my experience with all other patients I had treated, I found myself, when I first started to treat him, talking with colleagues about the case, as I said earlier. When analysts speak to colleagues of a particular case, they know they are trying to resolve a problem of their own that has been revived by something the patient said or did.

As I analyzed my need to talk about Reginald, I got in touch with two important wishes. For one, I was teasing my colleagues the way Reginald was teasing me. I placed them in an uncomfortable position as they listened to and identified with me. But there was a second, more important, wish behind my need to bring up the case so constantly. I recognized it only in hindsight: If I talked to enough people about my patient, perhaps someone would recognize who he was and give me his name.

As I experienced frustration, I occasionally observed paranoid reactions in myself. I was wondering, "Who *is* this man, really?" A few colleagues also became somewhat paranoid as I kept discussing the case. They warned of possible danger to me in treating him. I was frightened at times when I wondered about his true identity. But my fear of being murdered diminished as I realized he was interested in teasing me, not murdering me.

Several times in my work with him a favorite childhood story, "Rumpelstiltskin," came to mind. In that folk tale a miller falsely brags to the king that his daughter can spin straw into gold. The king incarcerates the girl in a room until she can spin a large quantity of gold. Helpless and in a panic, the girl is saved by an elf who says he will spin the gold for her if she promises to give him her firstborn. The elf spins the gold and the young woman is set free by the king, but she then changes her mind about giving the elf her child. The elf finally agrees to forego the firstborn, providing she can guess his name. When she says "Rumpelstiltskin," correctly naming him, the elf exclaims, "The devil told you that!" In his anger he stamps his right foot so hard that his whole leg sinks into the ground. A moment later he pulls at the left foot so hard that he tears himself in two.

There seemed to be several similarities between this folk tale and the case of Reginald Sheffield, especially the guessing of a name withheld. Reginald's analytic treatment, however, kept him from destroying himself as the "devil" turned into something of a savior.

As I worked with Reginald, I admitted to myself that at different times I felt like the elf, the miller's daughter, the miller, and the king. I also felt pleasure at the thought I had been able to relieve the anxiety and guilt eating away at this very intelligent but conflicted man. I knew his wife and children would be happier because he knew himself better. He would build the rest of his life upon what he gained through his analysis.

3

SOMETIMES I FEEL LIKE A DIRTY OLD MAN
The Woman Who Tried to Seduce Me

A beautiful—and I do not use the word lightly—twenty-nine-year-old woman, slim, with dark brown hair that fell in soft curls to her shoulders, stood at the door. She wore an expensive tailored dress of blue and green print that fell in soft folds to her knees. A wide-brimmed straw hat of deeper green suited the spring season. The heels on her black patent leather pumps were three inches high.

She had informed me during a phone conversation that she had been married for eight years and was the mother of a four-year-old boy. She also said she had been in treatment with another therapist. I knew this, for he had called me and confessed that for the first time he had allowed himself to be sexually seduced by a patient. He gave me her name,

Susan Brown, and said she lived in a fashionable community in New Jersey.

He explained that he could no longer treat her and asked if I could. He was an M.D. and did not want his colleagues to know of the affair. He had suggested she see me, a nonmedical psychoanalyst with a doctorate in social work. He knew I had treated several therapists, both M.D.'s and non-M.D.'s, who had had affairs with patients. I had helped them understand why they engaged in these forbidden alliances, an absolute no-no for any therapist.

"I'm so glad you could see me, Dr. Strean." Susan Brown's voice was soft, seductive, her blue eyes ablaze with friendliness.

I gestured toward a chair; she glided over on those highest of heels and lowered herself into it like a dancer.

Without a moment's delay she dove right into the sexual waters. "Dr. Strean, I know that Gregg"—the pseudonymous analyst—"has told you of our affair. I'm thoroughly enjoying it, but my relationship with my husband and son is suffering, and Greg feels I should break off with him and continue analysis with you."

She added wistfully, "I have never had much sexual satisfaction with my husband. He seemed loving before our marriage, but soon after the wedding he started to treat me coldly. Now he doesn't appeal to me, at least not the way Greg does. Greg is giving and warm. He gets inside my soul."

I thought, if she feels he gets inside her soul, she certainly would be receptive to his getting inside her body.

She then asserted, "I know patients are not supposed to have sex with their analysts, but I don't feel my affair has caused any conflict. I'm upset because I want to leave my husband and son. That's the reason I came for help. Not to get out of the affair with Greg."

For a patient, to have an affair with an analyst is exciting; I could see in Susan's first interview that this was a triumph she relished. I also knew that though she felt loved she also felt guilty at having turned the treatment into an affair so important she wanted to leave her family.

I had other thoughts, too. I could understand why my colleague had broken a sacrosanct rule: Susan was beautiful and seductive and engaging; she radiated an unusually attractive warmth. She reminded me of the first girl I ever had a crush on, a girl whose face and body had sexually aroused me when I was fourteen. She had also frightened me, though, because my erotic feelings were so overwhelming. I never acted on my feelings for Florence; the best I could do was tutor her in Latin. As I talked with Susan Brown, I recalled that when I first saw Florence, my family had just moved from Canada to the United States. Suddenly flooded with memories of Florence, I felt stimulated by the very thought of her. I was also stimulated by my new patient, but I kept the "hands off" policy firmly in mind.

Several times as Susan talked I fantasied making love to her. I not only empathized with my unfortunate colleague but envied him as well. Florence, in my adolescence, had been romantically involved with a boy named Marvin, and I had envied him. Now, thirty years later, in the first interview with Susan Brown, my oedipal drama was revived. Treatment would be in essence another Latin lesson, while Greg, like Marvin, enjoyed all the fun.

As I listened to Susan, I thought of what had happened in her therapy sessions with Greg—what analysts call "the erotic transference." The analyst uses this technical term to gain emotional distance when a patient falls passionately in love with him, as many patients do—women with male analysts, men with female analysts, and some with analysts of the same sex.

Freud was well aware of the discomfort, anxiety, and stimulation an analyst could feel when a woman patient fell in love with him. My own feeling is that Freud wrote in detail about the erotic transference because he was tempted to accede to it on one or more occasions. He refrained because he understood his own countertransference and knew that an affair would only harm the patient. He knew that such a sexual liaison was comparable to incest. He also knew it could be even more damaging in that the patient who came to him for relief from her suffering would be victimized even more if she became sexually involved with the analyst.

Yet I have often felt it is ridiculous to dismiss a woman patient's show of love with the interpretation that she really desires her father. Analysts, myself included, can defend themselves with such interpretations, or they can change the subject, or they can sink into profound silence. But the helpful analyst, in the spirit of Freud, aids the patient by asking her to verbalize her fantasies. Only then can she face unresolved childhood conflicts.

Why, if the patient is eager to have sex with the analyst, does the analyst not gratify her wish? There are several valid reasons. First, such gratification turns analysis into a love affair. This interferes with, and sometimes destroys, all chances of the patient's psychological growth. A love affair, while perhaps temporarily gratifying to both patient and analyst, never leads to inner change for the patient. Furthermore, as patients who have had sexual liaisons with therapists point out, analysts do not have any particular expertise as lovers. They are probers of the mind, not the body. An analyst is trained to do psychoanalysis; he holds no diploma in lovemaking.

Another serious consequence of such a liaison is that sooner or later the patient may want more than an affair. Most analysts are not prepared to marry their patients, so the affair usually makes the patient feel rejected and exploited.

Virtually every patient perceives the analyst as a parental figure. As a result, most of these sexual liaisons are mutually unsatisfactory because both parties are unconsciously involved in an incestuous relationship and the resultant guilt usually prevents pleasurable sex. Incidentally, I made a study of therapists who came to me for help because they were involved sexually with patients. Most of them reported that when they embarked on the affair they felt deeply depressed, unhappy with their marriages, or disillusioned with themselves or with life in general.

As I thought of my future work with Susan, I recalled clinical experiences with women who had strong erotic transferences. Many times an analyst is so overwhelmed by a patient's falling in love with him that he forgets to delve psychologically with the patient into what this behavior means to her. It can hold many meanings for the patient; it can be a bid for reassurance, a cover-up for hostility, an attempt to demean the analyst by taking him out of his professional role, a wish to be nurtured (turning the sexual experience into the earliest childhood wish to be fed at the breast), a defense against homosexuality, or all of these at different times in the analysis.

It was not possible with Susan, as it is not possible with any patient, to tell in advance the meaning her erotic feelings had at the moment. Very early in training, I learned that each patient has to be understood in terms of her unique past, her unique experiences throughout life, and her unique ways of coping.

An erotic transference is hard to handle, for me and for most analysts, I believe, because many patients, if their sexual demands are not gratified pronto, become vindictive and make threats, including suicide. But no matter how stimulated and excited the analyst may feel, no matter how badly he wants to avoid hurting the patient's feelings, he must say no to anyone insisting on immediate sexual gratification.

While the wish to express erotic feeling is always present, in this instance the patient is not saying, "I have a wish I want to understand," but "I must have you sexually or I might kill you or kill myself or ruin you or ruin myself because I will be so furious if you refuse me."

It is always difficult to say no to someone who insists on yes, and at the same time the analyst wants to prevent the patient from feeling guilty about her sexuality, but he *has* to say, in essence, "You cannot gratify your sexual wishes with me." The danger here is that the patient may unconsciously assume this means her sexual desire for anyone else is also forbidden.

I add parenthetically that most, if not all, of the sexually demanding patients I have treated feel very guilty about their sexual desires, and many of them lack a fulfilling sexual life. Thus the analyst has to say no to a wish he wants the patient to feel is natural--accepting the fulfillment of her erotic drive. One of the major tasks in any analysis is to liberate the sexual instinct, but like the good parent with the growing child, the analyst tries to help the patient accept sexual impulses without the need always to gratify them at once.

This is one lesson of all analyses: that we cannot always immediately have what we want. There is no doubt that intense erotic transferences make heavy demands on the therapist, but for an analyst to accede to a patient's sexual demands, as Greg did, is destructive to the patient and to the analyst as well. As I pointed out above, however, to ignore the sexual demand is almost equally destructive, for the analyst is thereby saying to the patient, "You are not a sexual person to me." This is a painful rejection and often an untrue statement, but it is a far more practical way of handling the situation.

The truth often is, as it was in Susan's case, that the analyst finds the patient sexually appealing but knows that for her good as well as his own there can be no sex between them. The patient over time must slowly accept this. The therapist cannot just say it once, she may have to hear it many times before she finally accepts it.

Susan, who came to therapy three times a week, seemed troubled at first about telling her husband she wanted to leave him. She also expressed guilt about taking Greg away from his wife. She alluded to other problems, such as being unable to enjoy sex with her husband. She told me she'd had two affairs prior to her marriage. Her relationships with men always started with her falling "madly in love," but she would lose interest in the man after several sexual "encounters," as she called them, eventually would come to loathe him, and finally would leave him. She felt this way with her husband, and I wondered if she would soon feel the same way toward Greg.

This pattern of "falling in love," then becoming tired of and angry at the previously loved one, was true of Susan's relations to both men and women. She would build a close, warm relationship with a woman, wind up arguing, then feel indifferent. As I listened to her describe her major *modus vivendi*, I wondered when she would fall in love with me and how and when she would reject me. She seemed to follow this pattern with everyone in her life.

Knowing Susan was a woman who eventually ran away from a man induced in me some interesting countertransference problems. As an adolescent I was always challenged by the woman who held herself back, and Susan reminded me of Florence, not only because she was beautiful and filled with energy but also because she withheld herself from me. Just as I had been challenged at fourteen and on other occasions, I was now challenged by a patient. I told myself that Susan would eventually leave me. How, I wondered, could I keep her?

The interest in a woman who is hard to get and hard to keep is an old story for psychoanalysts. Such a woman is really the "mother" no child ever fully gets to keep for himself but who always seems enticing. Like the Mona Lisa's smile, she is both seductive and rejecting. Susan was my Mona Lisa of the moment. She stimulated me, excited me, but I knew she was prepared to get rid of me if I allowed her to become the temporary oedipal victor.

I was challenged, but I was also aware of traps into which I could fall with this enticing woman. She revealed such a trap to me one morning when she confessed, "I was seduced not only by Greg but by two other therapists as well. I really try to be a good patient, but something happens when these men want me sexually. I know it's no help to me to screw my analysts, but they get to me."

She tried to present herself as a victim of circumstance, and concomitantly I realized she possessed a very limited amount of insight into her wish to turn the therapeutic relationship into a fleeting love affair—a coup on the couch.

For her first six sessions, however, she seemed to take therapy seriously. She produced many thoughts, and she free associated to her dreams, fantasies, and past history like a well-trained patient. As she talked, she reflected, again like a well-trained patient, on her relationship with her father. "He was a very cold, unavailable, and distant man," she said. "My mother was critical and demanding but endlessly seductive toward him, and I think most of the time this turned him off."

Her dreams and fantasies centered on the theme of searching everywhere for a man—a father who would love only her—but finding each man unresponsive. I had the impression during these first sessions she was trying to please me, to cooperate with me. To give me what I wanted to hear—dreams, fantasies, childhood memories, the stuff of which an analyst's dreams are made.

I also had the feeling she was working hard to impress me instead of facing her own conflicts. I even felt mild irritation because I sensed she was trying to manipulate me, giving an apple to the teacher rather than free associations to an analyst.

Then, in her seventh session, Susan suddenly changed her approach. She threw herself on the couch, said accusingly, "You're really a very cold man. Just like my father." Then plaintively, tears starting to flow: "Couldn't you be a little warmer? Couldn't you show some love?"

Her plea for love induced a variety of feelings in me. On one level I felt sorry for her, as I always feel sorry for anyone in tears. I felt the impulse to gratify this seemingly deprived child who appeared in distress and craved love. Had I seen her earlier in my career, before I'd had so much personal analysis, I actually might have tried to be warmer and more giving. But now I knew better. Any woman who had successfully seduced three therapists couldn't be that deprived. On the contrary, Susan was acting like a clever child, trying to make me feel sorry for her so she could more easily seduce me.

The best approach at this time was to explore the conflicts causing her over-intense wish for love. I asked, "What are you feeling that makes you want warmth and love from me?"

She burst into a rage. "That's a stupid question!" she snapped. "It's like asking somebody who is thirsty why he wants water. You're really a cold potato." Then she propelled herself off the couch and without another word walked out of my office.

At that moment I felt many emotions. On the one hand I felt the impulse to shout after her, "You spoiled brat, sit down and behave yourself. You want what you want when you want it and if you don't get it you throw a temper tantrum." But I also felt some doubts about myself. Was I too rejecting, too limiting? Maybe Susan was right—I was a cold potato. (I had been compared to many things but never to a potato.)

Like all analysts, I am often the butt of patients' intense anger. Though I know no analysis can be successful without such displays of anger, I always feel a certain tension—a normal reaction—in the face of hostility or disapproval.

I studied my reaction to Susan after she walked out of the office. I thought of the time I had felt dismissed and unloved by my mother or by other women in my life. Susan triggered my greatest vulnerability as a human being and my greatest limitation as an analyst: when I feel rejected, I respond in one of two ways. Sometimes I ask, What's wrong with me? What does that person disapprove of? Like a child whose parents do not love him. At other times I want to attack the person for not loving me—how dare he? I felt both feelings with Susan. On the one hand I wondered, How have I misbehaved? On the other hand, I thought, that bitch. She doesn't love me the way she should.

My feelings toward Susan were those of a guilty, rejected little boy and, at the same time, those of a boy who wanted to kick his mother in the teeth for not loving him. These reactions are triggered in all of us when we feel unwanted. Only after many years of personal analysis was I able to acknowledge the child in me, to be aware of my little boy reactions. Then, much later in life, I learned to withstand the verbal abuse of my patients as they transferred their outrage to me.

I have rarely heard analysts acknowledge their discomfort in the face of massive hostility and rejection by patients, but I believe analysts would suffer fewer heart attacks if they could admit that, even though they know the abuse is just a transference, it can still hurt. No matter how mature an analyst or anyone else becomes, the child within is always alive and susceptible to anger and pain.

At Susan's next session she apologized for her "performance" and said, "I know you want to help me." For the following several sessions she talked of how she had lacked approval and emotional warmth from her father, who was always away on business trips or out playing poker "with the boys."

A few sessions later she spoke again of her yearning for a warm, loving father, then suddenly asked, "Will you hold me close for just a little while?" She added hastily, "For reassurance."

She was presenting herself once more as a deprived little girl neglected by a cold father. My subjective reaction was similar to the one I had felt earlier in her treatment: I felt sorry for her, wanted to gratify her wish, but had to refuse her request. Then I wondered, as I have before and since, if I was in the right profession.

In response to her plea to hold her, I asked, "What are you feeling and thinking that makes you want physical assurance at this moment?"

She raised her slim body, clad in black silk, from the couch, and announced defiantly, "I'm leaving forever." She walked out the door.

Susan did not appear for her next three sessions. She did call to leave messages on my answering machine, however: "You no-good son of a bitch. You have an icy personality. You sure are a cold potato," and so forth. I was to hear that description of myself throughout her analysis.

During her absence I felt a vast array of emotions. I wanted to lash out at her for making me feel so impotent and ineffective, so deserted, so abandoned. Though the conscious, rational part of my ego told me Susan was behaving like an angry, impulsive child who wanted to hurt me when she did not get her way, I faced the fact that a part of me was raging because I was not getting *my* way.

Analysts have to be ready for all eventualities, including desertion by patients, yet during Susan's absences I found myself reliving a very painful part of my childhood. This explained my intense anger and mild to moderate depression at her failure to appear.

When I was between five and eight, my mother sometimes punished me by saying, "If you don't behave, I'll send you to a reformatory." She occasionally went so far as to pack my suitcase for such a journey. I knew a reformatory was a school for bad boys, a place where dreadful things went on, and I tried my best to behave. As a child I never knew whether my mother was serious, but these threats made me feel depressed and furious at her. This is precisely how I felt with Susan. I was not sure whether she was just threatening to leave—throwing her weight around to scare me, as my mother did—or really meant she was through.

I got in touch with the little boy in me, the child who saw Susan as a mother, the child who was begging, "Please don't leave me, I need you," but who was also raging, "Mother, I want to kill you for not loving me." Thereafter I could see Susan more realistically.

During one of her message calls I picked up the phone, said, "This is Dr. Strean."

After a silence she asked, "Will you still see me?"

"I've been keeping your hour open because I wasn't sure of your plans," I said quietly.

I felt great relief when she said, "I'll be there next Monday."

I was no longer defeated; I could once again work with my challenging patient (un-really my challenging mother and challenging girlfriend). When I found myself elated about Susan's return, I realized it was as though my mother were saying, "I'm not sending you away. Let's make up." But I knew if I conveyed any sign of pleasure to Susan she would torment me with more threats. I was in another classic analytic dilemma: I felt happy she was behaving the way I wanted her to, but I knew that to show much joy would only reinforce her infantile behavior, gratify her childish fantasies.

For me, it has never been easy to accept a patient's threat to quit treatment, and I doubt it is easy for any analyst. Not only is there potential loss of income but inevitably the analyst asks himself, Did I do something wrong? Could I have done something more effectively? The anxiety and self-questioning I experienced in the early years of my practice still lingers on when a patient threatens to walk out. I have frequently likened psychoanalysis to playing golf: you can always better your score; there is always room for improvement.

Having a patient threaten to abandon treatment is a bit like having a spouse threaten to leave a marriage. Being an analyst is quite different from being a spouse, of course, but there are similarities between an analytic relationship and a marriage. In both, two human beings form a partnership and try to live with each other. Each must make certain accommodations to the other, and the potential for conflict is strong. Just as most husbands and wives at one time or another are convinced they deserve a better partnership, so are most patients certain they deserve a "better" therapist. As a result, the threat to quit treatment maybe is not uncommon.

Although I'm sure many analysts have difficulty with this issue, I feel my own anxiety at the threat of separation is stronger than that of most of my colleagues. As with any psychological difficulty the reasons are, as we say in psychoanalysis, "overdetermined" meaning there are many reasons for the same act or the same symptom. One of those reasons comes immediately to mind and has to do with my father.

During the first twenty-one years of my life, my family moved eighteen times. Saying good-bye to friends, relatives, and neighbors was always a sad occasion for me, and I always felt angry that the permanent and familiar had suddenly been taken away from me. My father, when he felt frustrated, simply abandoned a situation. One time, for example, we moved to a new house because he did not like the sound of the dog barking next door. Another time we moved because a neighbor played the piano too loudly. My father was too afraid of his anger to confront those who frustrated him. He preferred instead to pack up all his possessions and move. My mother always complied, and I tended to identify with her and submit to my father's edicts, as did my sister.

Before my father became a bacteriologist, he practiced dentistry at an office in our home. I saw his dental chair lifted into a moving van seven or eight times, and each time wished it would break in two. This was obviously a revengeful fantasy toward my father for what I felt he was doing to me—breaking me in two emotionally. I also wanted the dental chair destroyed because my father was *my* dentist, and I hated his drilling and at times pulling my teeth. I reasoned if there were no dental chair I would be protected from such pain. In hindsight, I think he was probably as upset and fearful as I was, but I experienced him as a cruel sadist who was out to tear me apart.

Through my experience in warding off feelings of help-lessness, weakness, desperation, and anger when a patient threatens to leave, I have become an expert in dealing with such patients and I have helped other analysts salvage un-treatable cases. I am particularly sensitive to those conflicts that provoke patients to want to leave treatment.

Susan threatened to leave because I was not gratifying her desire to be loved continually and intensely. I was upset by her leaving me temporarily, but I felt that if I chased her, she would so enjoy the chase that she would constantly threaten to leave. I thought she would return if I did not beg her. Therefore, I did not call her when she skipped those three sessions. In other situations, however, I have phoned patients, because I was convinced they needed more than anything else a sign I wanted them to return. The reasons for termination and termination threats are many, and each person who threatens has to be responded to differently.

A few sessions after her return, Susan showed up with a proposal. She entered the room, walked to the chair, not the couch, and announced, "I want to stop this kind of treatment because I feel I'm not ripe for psychoanalysis. I think it would be a good idea to go into group therapy with another analyst. Instead of being in analysis with you, I'll be your friend."

She was once again trying to remove me from my role as analyst, turn me into a lover.

"What bothers you about being in analysis with me? You say you'd rather be my friend than my patient. Why?"

She replied, "I feel so beneath you as a patient. I can't stand your power over me. You seem like a big prick. I feel like a nothing, wiped out. The only way I can feel like a somebody is to get you to fall in love with me and go to bed with me."

Her statement was honest and I felt empathy toward her. She was admitting she could feel human only when she could get a man to fall in love with her. To show her that I understood, I said, "I realize it is hard for you to like yourself as my patient, that only if you seduce me will you feel like somebody."

She responded with a smile. "You are the most wonderful man I've ever known. You're kind. You're understanding. You're brilliant. And you have such sex appeal. I'm glad you're so dedicated to your profession and I respect you for what you're doing—trying to help me rather than screw me."

At first I was taken in by her turnabout. She seemed to say she loved me as an analyst, not a sex object, and I felt grateful. I was no longer a cold potato. She now believed I felt warmly toward her. I also felt proud of myself for having turned a promiscuous woman who seduced therapists into a cooperative patient.

Without another word she resumed her sessions on the couch. Between sessions I thought of her at times, realized there were moments I felt more like her boyfriend than her analyst. I finally realized she was one of the cleverest women I had ever met. She knew the way to my heart was to tell me what a fine analyst I was. All else having failed, she hoped this would make me love her.

I became more and more convinced that beneath Susan's compliments lay a powerful manipulative attitude. She sensed what each man wanted to hear and used this knowledge to try to get him in her grasp. Even her dreams had a manipulative quality.

One night she dreamed she was applauding me as I received accolades at an analytic convention. The next night she dreamed my books were reviewed in the *New York Times* with the highest of praise. In her third dream I was elected president of the American Psychoanalytic Association. She figured out just those situations that would enhance my narcissism.

Had I been less experienced at the time, less aware of the fact that being preoccupied with a patient between sessions was a sign of unresolved countertransference, I might have succumbed to Susan's clever advances. I should also add that I had a few erotic dreams about her, but used those dreams to her therapeutic advantage, not to gratify my own feelings.

Eventually it became clear to me that Susan was not trying to understand herself through analysis. Instead, she was figuring out how to defeat me as an analyst. Having recognized this, I told her one day, "You are still working very hard to seduce me by telling me all the things you think I want to hear, rather than trying to understand your own conflicts."

She became infuriated. "You are a cold, hostile, arrogant man," she said. "You're very insensitive to a patient's needs. I want to rip you into twenty pieces. I would enjoy attending your funeral!" As she vented her anger session after session, I kept recalling Congreve's lines in the play *The Mourning Bride*: "Heaven has no rage like love to hatred turned, / Nor hell a fury like a woman scorned." Written in 1697, the words have never lost one iota of truth.

When she realized I was not going to retaliate with anger, Susan tried another ploy. She accused me of being a "weak, fragile man," of being intimidated by her. She said she would find an analyst who was "more potent." At the same time, however, I felt irritated by her attempt to make me jealous. I felt actually jealous and I pictured her leaving me, finding another analyst, rejecting me as a lover.

I decided to tell her this. I said, "You're trying to make me jealous."

She took this to mean I felt jealous and changed her attitude. "I didn't know you were capable of human emotion," she said. "I'm glad to know I can finally make you jealous."

She then told me that with all my dedication to psychoanalysis, I was "an understanding human being," for I could acknowledge human emotions in myself. Then she described her strong erotic fantasies about me. She talked about how much she would enjoy having my penis inside her, how much gratification my caressing her breasts would bring. She concocted some of the most seductive situations, fantasies, and wishes I have ever heard from a patient.

Though I knew her defenses well, I was moved by her soft voice and now more caring attitude toward me. Again I found myself feeling like quite a man. I felt I must be something of a Romeo if a woman as beautiful as Susan wanted me sexually. But as stimulated as I felt, I constantly reminded myself of how she used sexuality as a means of manipulation, a way of buttressing her shaky self-image and precarious self-esteem.

Once again I pointed this out to her and once again she became furious. But this time she did not walk out. She remained, and she started to face her own feelings, though it was a full year before she could accept the fact I was available to her only to help her understand herself.

The more I did not gratify her wishes, the more she could understand the childhood dramas and dreams she was trying to act out with me. She finally realized they focused on her "stimulating but withdrawing" father, who had left her feeling, in her words, "high and dry sexually." This was what she had wanted to do with me and other men—leave them "high and dry" as revenge against her frustrating father. She acted out with them what she saw as the tragedy of her sexual life. At the same time she unconsciously got even with her father, since each man represented him.

Susan finally realized she was more at war with men than in love with them, as she had thought. Her wish for vengeance against her father for not making her his true love had dominated much of her emotional life as well as her behavior toward men. She also realized she had mimicked her very seductive mother, who occasionally managed to win her husband's erotic attention.

As Susan began to focus more on her internal conflicts and became less concerned about seducing me, her marriage improved and her relationship with her son became more loving. She ended the affair with Greg (I had known this would occur as each became more fully analyzed).

Through my work with Susan I became more empathic toward those therapists who abdicate their therapeutic role to become lovers of patients. Had I been less experienced and less thoroughly analyzed, however, I wonder whether Susan might not have succeeded in adding me to her list of lovers, thus helping me fail as a psychoanalyst.

4

THE PATIENT WHO HATED ME
The Case of the Anti-Semite

It follows like the night the day that every psychoanalyst sooner or later will be the recipient of every patient's intense hostility. This hostility emerges for many reasons. More often than not, patients become angry because the analyst does not praise them, does not offer enough interpretations, or because, as one patient put it, "It's just too darn quiet!"

Patients frequently experience the analyst's silence as rejection. The analyst appears not to care about the patient's aches and pains, seems to be preoccupied with concerns of his own. Inasmuch as every one of us longs for affection, needs support, and secretly yearns for a loving, nurturing parent, which every patient hopes the analyst will be, it is no surprise one of the most frequent complaints is that the analyst is too silent and seems uninterested.

But anger toward the analyst may stem from a variety of other sources as well. A wife who constantly complains her husband is cold and passive, for example, may grow furious when her analyst points out that her dreams and fantasies show she has unconsciously sought a cold, aloof husband because she is frightened of a warm, assertive man. Or a husband who complains that his wife's constant criticism keeps him from feeling sexual may grow furious when he is informed that he wishes to be a little boy seeing his wife as a mother who, by criticizing him, prevents him from feeling sexual. Patients get angry when they are confronted with the fact that they have unconsciously arranged their own misery. They frequently hate the analyst for showing them this reality. As children they may have been victims of their parents' neurotic conflicts but as adults they will feel better and function better as they understand how they keep themselves children and make a spouse, colleague, or friend into the parent of the past. Yet most of my patients become quite angry with me when I point out they love to collect injustices of the past and present. As I show them they derive gratification out of making themselves deprived children. At times like this, they may see the world as a collection of hostile ogres and the analyst as the cruelest ogre of them all.

I have discovered another reason patients hate their analysts. Each patient expects the analyst to be the perfect parent. Eventually, however, the therapist will become, in the patient's mind, the imperfect parent of the past. Then on his head will be heaped all the hatred the patient dared not feel or express for his own parent when he was a child.

I have often told students and colleagues that if an analysis goes on without the patient expressing hatred toward the analyst, something is wrong with the analysis. Either the analyst is subtly squelching the patient's rage or the patient is too frightened to be himself and say what really irks him. Rage is to be expected, because in the analytic situation wishes are always being frustrated and habitual rationalizations and justifications constantly questioned.

One of the most powerful reasons for the hostility of patients is the puncturing of their expectations. When a person first enters analysis he is the recipient of an unconditional, positive regard, careful listening, and concern. Most patients, most of the time, are pleased with the analyst's attitude. They feel understood and loved; their self-esteem rises. They enjoy the rare opportunity of not being censured for hostile or sexual fantasies. Their guilt thus diminishes, they feel loved, and they love the analyst. They feel like forgiven children who are very much cared for, regardless of how bad their behavior has been.

Reuben Fine has referred to this initial phase of analysis as the "honeymoon." During this period all seems wonderful, and both parties feel almost ecstatic.

But every honeymoon eventually ends. Fantasies become punctured, hopes and expectations are not gratified, and bliss recedes. Anyone who expects bliss to be everlasting will be keenly disappointed, then angry.

Shakespeare was well aware of this when he had Richard II say, "Sweet love, I see, changing his property, Turns to the sourest and most deadly hate." The moment when "sweet love" turns to "deadly hate" is a trying time for both patient and analyst. It is trying for the patient because he thought he was going to find paradise, live in that Garden of Eden that had always eluded him. It is trying for the analyst because, after being revered, he is suddenly derogated. Many patients threaten to quit treatment after the analytic honeymoon ends, and some actually do.

While hostility in the analytic situation takes different forms and has different causes, I have found that it reaches its most intense and most pervasive form right after the honeymoon. Different patients express their disappointments in various ways: some arrive late, some forget to pay their bills, others fall ill and miss sessions, still others refuse to talk, and many verbally demean the analyst.

Usually the patient chooses a form of anger that has

served him in the past. If threatening to run away from relationships has worked for him, he will threaten to leave treatment. If sulking and pouting has gotten results, he will sulk and pout at the analyst. If he has been successful at manipulating others by withholding words or money, this he will try with the analyst.

How the analyst reacts to the patient's hostility has much to do with how secure or vulnerable the analyst feels in the face of the form of anger the patient shows. I have never been too upset when patients display anger by arriving late, not paying fees, or making derogatory remarks. I have never taken these forms of hostility personally because I have rarely used them in coping with my own frustrations.

But one issue on which I feel very vulnerable is anti-Semitism. I find it difficult to maintain my empathy for and continue to offer benign understanding to a patient who hates me because I am Jewish.

This occurred when I worked with Joseph Sullivan, an account executive in New York City who came to see me when he was thirty-five. Almost six feet tall, weighing just under two hundred pounds, he proved to be a man with a slow stride and a quiet manner. Though successful in his work, he said he felt very depressed much of the time. He had poor relationships in general with both men and women. He did not date often, believing women would reject him, as many had. At times, he confessed, he thought of suicide.

Joe, as he said he wished to be called, also admitted he was ashamed of his background. He was a college graduate with an M.A. in business administration from Columbia University, but his father drove a taxi and had never finished high school. His mother was "just a housekeeper" and "a limited woman who read only true romance magazines." He had a younger brother who had failed academically, and two sisters whom he described contemptuously as "emotional cripples."

Before coming to me, Joe had consulted several other therapists. He described them as men who seemed responsible but could not help him. When I questioned him about his previous therapists, it became clear, as it usually does with patients who have had several therapists, that Joe felt a latent contempt for and anger at these therapists and unconsciously wanted to defeat them.

But he seemed to take an immediate liking to me. He told me I was different from his previous therapists: "You spend most of the time listening and trying to understand me instead of talking at me. And I think that's terrific."

Over the next few sessions he spoke about his anger as a child toward his parents and siblings and as an adult toward colleagues and friends. Because I did not censure him, his depression seemed to diminish. He started to like himself more and seemed to approve of me.

Our honeymoon lasted five months. During that time he dated women who did not walk out on him. He made more money at work, bought expensive, attractive clothes. He had no trouble, as he sometimes did before, in performing sexually. But, as is true with all honeymoons, Joe's eventually ended.

One day during the sixth month of treatment he had missed an appointment, giving no excuse. I said, "In the future, I'll have to charge you for missed appointments."

He was lying on the couch and he turned in my direction. In a voice that rang with anger, this man—who not so long ago had told me, "You're the greatest guy who ever lived"— now said, "You cheap, dirty Jew bastard! You're only interested in money. You use psychoanalysis like a whorehouse to charge patients large sums of money so they get a little bit of love."

While I had never told Joe, as I feel no need to tell any patient, about my religious background, he assumed he knew it. He went on, "I don't think I can be associated with somebody as greedy and selfish as you."

Still intensely angry, he ranted on, "Hitler was right! Someone like you should be exterminated for being a combination pimp and whore."

No patient had ever expressed this depth of hostility to me, and though I prided myself on my ability to accept any put-down with equanimity, I found Joe's remarks difficult to bear. As a boy growing up in Montreal, nine times out of ten if I found myself in any altercation it was because I was "Jewish." At times I was the victim of anti-Semitic gangs out to hurt and maim other children simply because they were Jewish. At school, where I earned high grades, my academic success sparked envy, and I heard myself occasionally referred to by both boys and girls as a "goddamn Jew bastard."

At the time I lived in Montreal, anti-Semitism was acute. I recall seeing signs in parks, "Gentiles Only." To get into McGill University in those days, Jewish students had to achieve 100 points higher than non-Jews on the matriculation examination. Growing up Jewish induced in me much ambivalence and intense emotion. On the one hand, I felt furious about this irrational discrimination and wanted to destroy my tormentors. On the other hand, I felt secretly apologetic and angry that I was Jewish, and I envied those who were not Jewish and could escape such unjustified vilification and hostility.

As I carefully explored this issue in my personal analysis, I realized I tended to associate being Jewish with feeling weak and vulnerable. Intelligent, yes, but not very masculine or competent.

And when Joe called me a "no-good Jew bastard," a part of me experienced him as a bully from childhood who hurt me unmercifully. Because of his height and weight, he could easily have beaten me up. He told me at one point, "You look like a weakling," and next to him I felt like one.

As he pounded away, his verbal assaults felt like physical blows. My heart beat faster, I felt sweaty, and I fantasied kicking him in the groin, feelings I had experienced as a boy when the gangs assaulted me. I thought of saying to Joe, "I really don't know if I can help you, I feel so incompetent."

Fortunately for me as an analyst, when I feel vulnerable and threatened, I tend to keep quiet. I remained silent as he continued his harangue, calling me a hungry capitalist more interested in his money than relieving his suffering.

I started to reflect on the times when my Gentile classmates had derided me for getting high grades. I felt the same conflict with Joe. On the one hand, I knew I was correct as analyst to listen quietly to his anti-Semitic venom, and this knowledge provided me with some comfort. On the other hand, I felt maligned and hated in many ways; I would have preferred to have his love rather than his hatred. This was similar to how I had felt in the face of the anti-Semitism in school, where I was berated for following the rules. I enjoyed earning high grades, but I hated being condemned because I was Jewish.

During the following session I had to listen to another outpouring of hatred from Joe. When he mocked me by speaking with a Jewish accent, I fumed silently and had strong fantasies of hurling him out of my office. Since I'd never before considered throwing a patient out of the office, I had to analyze in depth what this wish meant to me.

As I examined my desire to get rid of Joe, I thought again of the time in my life when I was most conflicted about being Jewish. When I was in high school, I applied to several colleges and was told these colleges had quotas for Jewish students. If I was accepted, I would be part of a restricted minority. I had secret fantasies, about which I told no one, of wanting to fake my application, to say I was Gentile, for which I have often been taken—in other words, to get rid of my Jewishness and Jewish identity.

I realized that by getting rid of Joe, I would be trying to rid myself of a part of myself that I apparently did not like.

I believe strongly that when analysts get rid of a patient, they frequently are trying to get rid of a part of themselves they cannot bear. All of us, when we strongly repudiate another person, are trying magically to dump on him something in ourselves we cannot accept.

When I was with Joe, what did I feel about myself that I could not tolerate, that made me want to get rid of him? Part of his customary paranoid demeanor caused him constantly to refer to Jews as "overambitious, overcompetitive, egocentric, self-serving, and narcissistic." These are qualities that, when I have seen them in myself, I have tried to repudiate, and most of the time I have been reasonably successful in doing so. The way I conduct my life personally and professionally allows me to think of myself generally as a warm, compassionate human being who believes in a "live and let live" philosophy. But Joe had me against the psychic ropes.

Like anyone who takes somebody else's accusations to heart, I could infer there was an element of truth to them— if not, then why was I so angry? Joe was forcing me to look once more at that part of me which was ambitious, competitive, and narcissistic and to recognize that, like all human beings, I had my selfishness, my mean thoughts and unsublimated aggression, and my residue of childhood narcissism.

While everything Joe was saying about me referred to unacceptable parts of himself, there were elements of truth in his projections that did apply to me. It would have been easy for me to say, "Everything you're accusing me of is part of your anti-Semitic paranoid subjective demeanor," and leave it at that. But Joe's accusations troubled me, and I had to face the reason.

I had to do with Joe what, for me, is one of the most difficult tasks of an analyst: to become objective and nonjudgmental about behavior that personally upset me. It is easy to be neutral, objective, empathic about attitudes and behavior that stir only limited conflicts. For example, I don't remember ever wanting to throw out a patient with a sexual conflict or a dependency problem or an extramarital problem. These issues have rarely made me feel vulnerable, but anti-Semitism did, and probably would again.

Empathizing with what I personally abhor has been for me one of the most trying dimensions of being a psychoanalyst. I recalled having had similar difficulty working with parents who abused their children and spouses who acted sadistically toward each other.

As I listened to Joe vilify me, I realized I was being forced into one of the most difficult tasks of my life—the need to empathize with a Hitler, for that was what Joe represented to me. Hitler was someone who wanted to kill me and whom I wanted to see killed. But Joe also represented, I realized, something else difficult to face: the Hitler in me.

Often in my personal analysis I mentioned a nightmare from which I woke in terror during World War II when I was six years old. In the nightmare, Hitler marched into my bedroom to haul me to a concentration camp. I felt terrified as he moved toward me to take me away from my home in Canada to what meant death in Germany. At the last moment of the nightmare, my father entered, ordered Hitler to leave me alone, and Hitler vanished. I woke up, feeling that I'd been rescued.

I often referred to this dream because it held several meanings. For one, it was a punishment dream of the sort that many boys have at age six—punishment for oedipal feelings. Hitler stood for my father, intent on punishing me for my incestuous fantasies and for competing with him. Yet my father also protected me from being hurt. As I examined the dream further, realizing each part of a dream is part of the dreamer, I had to face the times I had wished to act like Hitler, had to recognize my murderous wish to wipe out anyone who did not gratify all my wishes.

Despite my efforts to repudiate it, Joe and I were brothers

under the skin. As a child and as an adult, I'd had fantasies of wiping out those who stopped me from achieving what I wanted. Similarly, Joe, in his analysis, wanted to destroy me for stopping him from achieving what he wanted—to delay paying me, or not pay at all, for the sessions. The child in us wants everything to be a gift. Joe's analytic honeymoon had ended. He was out for the kill because I did not please him in the ways he deemed I should.

He felt thwarted when I asked him to pay for a session he did not attend. I was no longer the loving, all-giving father who would accept everything he did. For this he wanted to murder me. Though it was difficult, I began to empathize with Joe. I, too, had felt like a Hitler when I was not as loved as I would have liked to be or cared for in all the ways I thought I should have been.

As I began to identify more with Joe, feel the anti-Semite in myself, I became more compassionate, less angry, and more desirous of helping him. My experience with Joe reaffirmed for me that to help a patient psychoanalytically, you have to step into his shoes, feel what he feels, and understand these feelings as fully as possible. I began to see that Joe's anti-Semitism was a function of unrealized ambition, jealousy, lack of gratification, and the belief that I was treating him badly because I would not give him a free session—feelings I had experienced. The better I understood him, the more I could help him.

As I silently became more empathic and less angry, on some level Joe felt my emotional availability. His rage diminished as my rage diminished. His wish to examine himself increased as I wished to examine his conflicts more deeply and as I concomitantly explored my own. He no longer hurled accusations but looked more deeply into his feelings about women, his parents, his siblings.

One day during the latter part of his first year of treatment he described a dream in which he stood on Orchard Street, a Jewish section on New York's Lower East Side. As he looked around, he woke up suddenly. As I listened to his associations to the dream, it was clear he was trying to get closer to me but could not tolerate the idea and thus had wakened abruptly. To Joe, getting close to me meant accepting me not only as a Jew but also as a person. It was becoming apparent as we moved along in the analysis that our work was stirring up in Joe homosexual fantasies which he found intolerable.

At an appropriate time in the analysis I made the interpretation that Joe was afraid to feel close to me because this would mean he was sexually involved with me.

This frightened him, as I had known it would to some degree, and, his hostility returning (as it does when we fear anything), he said angrily, "You're a Jewish faggot. You probably want to seduce me."

Thus we entered Round 2 of Joe's anti-Semitic phase. It was apparent his extreme hatred was a defense against his long-buried homosexual wishes, which had prevented him from taking women seriously. By attacking me, he tried to protect himself against loving, sexual wishes.

As he realized I was not going to become defensive at his attacks, now focused on the charge I appeared to be "gay," he started to identify with my analytic attitude. He began to realize that, like everything else homosexuality was to be understood, rather than repudiated. Everyone, man and woman, has homosexual feelings, which are a residue from childhood when they did not differentiate between the sexes but simply wanted love from everyone.

As Joe felt more comfortable with his homosexual fantasies, he became friendlier toward me, since I did not present a danger to him. One day he dreamed he was wearing a yarmulke and a prayer shawl and standing in a synagogue drinking wine with Jewish men. In that dream he was quite the Jewish man himself, even with the name Sullivan.

In another session he talked of his secret wish to be Jewish. This, I believe, lies behind the vitriolic anger in all anti-

Semites. Why doth the gentleman protest too much unless he holds this underlying wish based on envy? Joe's picture of himself in a synagogue meant he was part of a warm, giving family. Wearing a skull cap and prayer shawl meant he was closer to God, an omnipotent father who takes care of all wishes. Jesus, who was a Jew, represents what many men wish to be—God's son. This wish came up several times in Joe's thoughts.

He began to feel more relaxed with me and experienced loving me as less threatening, even enriching. This attitude carried over to the other relationships in his life. He met a young woman who taught psychology in a city college. They fell in love and were married toward the end of his analysis. His new tolerance spread to his family, and he urged his two sisters to go into therapy. He made new friends in his office, some of whom were Jewish.

My work with Joe helped me understand the conflicts of other anti-Semitic patients whom I treated later. I recall a woman in analysis, a reporter on a city newspaper, who sometimes called me a yid, a derogatory word for Jew, and who flooded her hours with expressions of hatred for Jews. As her analysis moved along, it became clear, as it had with Joe, that she felt a secret love and admiration for Jews. Toward the end of treatment she married a Jewish physician whose first name and surname were similar to mine.

Thus the experience with Joe proved of great benefit both to him and to me. Because I did not allow myself to explode at his attacks, returning hate for hate, I learned more about myself and about my feelings of hatred for those who are "different" from me. Joe was able to face painful conflicts in himself, and by understanding them, he felt release from much fear and anger.

Psychoanalysis should always be a growth process for both analyst and patient. In the case of Joe, both of us became less judgmental and more loving.

5

WHAT PRICE SUCCESS?
The Physician Who
Turned Rebel

For most of my life, achievement has been for me a dominant passion, at times a passion that has felt like a horrendous compulsion. When I first consulted Reuben Fine to consider going into analysis with him, I told him that from time to time I felt two heavy weights, one on each shoulder, and wanted to get rid of them.

As I spoke in analysis of the fantasies connected with these two weights, I realized they were images of my mother and father pushing and pressuring me to come first in class, hit home runs on the ball field, and be a superstar in the Boy Scouts, at day camp, in the drama society, in Hebrew School, and in Sunday School.

I would say perhaps the most neurotic dimension of my personality is that unless I am successfully achieving, I start to worry about how worthwhile I am. To me, achieving is like being loved, and not achieving is like being a "dumb boy" and unloved.

My angriest and most anguishing memories involve times I was admonished for coming in third instead of first in class, hitting a single instead of a home run, and failing to win prizes in scholastic or athletic competitions. My books and articles are obviously "prizes" I wanted to work hard for. Emotionally I have used them from time to time to placate the voices within me that echo my parents' voices crying out, "Thou must produce!"

As I worked actively in my personal analysis on this conflict, I had an experience outside my office that exerted a powerful effect on me personally and on my work with patients. I was then in the process of toning down my childish wish for parental approval and love, and as a result, I was feeling less compulsion to succeed and produce. At this time I was invited to a Bar Mitzvah in Montreal. I looked forward to the Bar Mitzvah because it would give me a chance to renew my ties with family and friends I had not seen for several years.

Arriving at the synagogue, I was met by the Bar Mitzvah boy and his parents, who were close relatives of mine. They all appeared somber, pensive, anything but joyous. They confessed none of them had slept well the previous night. As I sensed their tension, I wanted somehow to help it diminish. I jokingly said to thirteen-year-old Robert, the celebrity of the day, "Maybe you'll fall asleep when they call you to the reading of the Torah."

His parents responded with admonishing glares, not appreciating my attempt at frivolity. But Robert laughed and said, "I may even faint." Which told me how frightened he felt. I had known for years that words of jest often mask intense feelings of fear. Jesting, telling jokes, and making puns have been my favorite means of dispelling my own anxiety.

An hour later, as the time drew near for Robert to perform,

I noticed that he became paler and paler until he looked more like a ghost than a happy star. His father was standing on the altar, and his mother was seated quite a distance from us, inasmuch as this was an Orthodox synagogue. I took it upon myself to try to comfort Robert.

I walked over to him and said, "You seem quite uncomfortable."

He responded in a low voice, "You're right. I think I'm either going to vomit or faint."

"Would you like to step outside for a few minutes and breathe some fresh air?"

I thought the four-degree weather of Montreal that day might revive Robert somewhat. But he said guiltily, "I'm going to be called up to read a portion of the Torah in about fifteen minutes. I better stay here."

I remarked spontaneously, "Your health is more important than a few minutes of singing from the Torah, which nobody understands anyway."

Robert looked at me gratefully. "I think I would like to go outdoors with you."

As we walked outside, I must have had two hundred free associations. I began to recall my own Bar Mitzvah. I felt the rage of having to start preparation at the age of six, when I went to Hebrew School three times a week to prepare to become a man seven years later. While standing outside the same synagogue where I had my Bar Mitzvah, I realized that, like me before him, Robert was not allowing himself to feel his anger as he underwent the same compulsory ritual. I thought that perhaps in a more poignant way the load on my shoulders, about which I had told my analyst, was the feeling of being a servant to my parents, my extended family, my Hebrew teachers, and all the others who had ordered, "*You must perform.*"

Obviously I was involved with Robert because I wanted to give him an experience for which I had yearned when I was thirteen. How I had longed to hear someone say, "You're angry at all the pressures on you. It's okay to be angry, and it's okay if you don't perform perfectly."

As I collected my associations, I thought how inappropriate it was to put so much pressure on any thirteen-year-old boy. A Bar Mitzvah ceremony would be more fitting for an eighteen-year-old than for a boy approaching puberty.

Robert clearly felt the same ambivalence toward the pressure that I had felt years ago. Realizing this, I asked, "Wouldn't you like to say to hell with the whole thing?"

He replied solemnly, "I've been preparing for this day for years. I'm worried I'll make a lot of mistakes."

I knew that when anyone, Bar Mitzvah boy or not, worried about making a mistake, there was an unconscious wish to make the mistake, to protest the duty he was commanded to carry out. I was also convinced that anybody who worries about not performing—and anyone who cannot perform—usually has strong unconscious wishes *not* to perform, to oppose parents or teachers.

With this in mind, and realizing fully how closely I identified with Robert, I told him, "Part of being a Bar Mitzvah, which means 'son of good deeds,' *is* making mistakes. I made several at my Bar Mitzvah ceremony, and I make several mistakes every day as an adult."

Robert said uneasily, "I'm scared of making mistakes, because my parents and everybody else will be sore at me."

I knew exactly how Robert felt: I had been there hundreds of times. I told him, "If your parents or anyone else gives you a hard time for making mistakes, they are acting like jerks. Any intelligent person knows you are supposed to make mistakes if you're a human being." I further reminded him, "The only people who don't make mistakes are corpses."

Robert looked at me half gratefully, half skeptically, but he appeared less nervous, and he clearly enjoyed hearing me verbalize the resentment he himself could not express.

Because he appreciated every word I uttered, I felt encouraged to share more of my thoughts: "You could have a

great life even if you didn't go through with this ritual."
"I know." He smiled. "But I have to."

I felt a strong rebellious satisfaction as I pictured Robert or myself, now one and the same, refusing to go through the Bar Mitzvah ceremony. His terror really arose from his deep wish to say the hell with it, but he was afraid to express his intense anger. It is not easy to oppose parents, grandparents, relatives, the tradition of centuries, a rabbi, and a cantor—not to mention an entire congregation. Robert, to me, was the part of myself that would have enjoyed at his age defying the world, which seemed such an exacting one.

I pointed out, referring to his rebellious wishes as well as my own, "Think how famous you'll be. The only kid in Canada, maybe all of North America, maybe all of the world, maybe the only boy in Jewish history, who had the guts to say, 'To hell with my bar Mitzvah. My feelings and my emotional health are more important!'"

Robert laughed with pleasure, then thoughtfully asked, "You really think it's okay to make mistakes?" He added half sadly, half matter-of factly, "I think I'll go ahead, but I'm sure I'm going to make lots of mistakes."

Hurrah, I said to myself, the kid is saying he will feel intact even if he makes mistakes. He's smiling and feeling better because he now believes it's all right to make mistakes. I identified so strongly with his feelings of relief that I pictured those heavy weights falling from my shoulders. I realized the walk with Robert was more therapeutic for me than for him, but I knew it had also been helpful to him.

With two minutes to go before Robert had to walk to the altar, I made a deal with him. I said, "I want to help you make mistakes. In addition to the gift I already gave, I will give you five dollars for every mistake you make."

He looked at me quizzically, as if I were a bit crazy, then said okay and shook my hand feebly.

As I returned to my seat, I felt elated. I realized I truly believed everything I'd said to Robert. I had conveyed to him that I would like him and respect him regardless of how many mistakes he made. I felt elated, too, because I realized that mistakes, or even failure, do not mean a person is worthless, castrated, or feeble. Part of the human condition *is* making mistakes.

Robert performed very well and enjoyed receiving ten extra dollars from me. I did not even notice the two mistakes, but he told me later he made them deliberately to get his reward. In hindsight, I think my actions that day might be called behavior modification—though few behavior modifiers reward their patients for making mistakes.

Despite Robert's success, his parents were angry when they learned what had happened between their son and me, and to this day they have not fully forgiven me. But I did not feel too upset—the experience with Robert was educational and had an extremely profound effect on us. I am sure we are both better human beings because of that experience. It is probably one of the few therapeutic Bar Mitzvahs on record, perhaps the only one.

As a result of my experience with Robert I began to appreciate how important it was to accept my own limitations, my own failures, with more equanimity, less self-punishment, less self-hatred, and less self-consciousness. This new awareness sharpened my therapeutic work with patients as I helped them accept that failure does not mean the end of the world but is part of living. "To err is human and also highly therapeutic," I reassured myself on many occasions.

My experience with Robert induced in me a profound conviction that a patient's failure to write the great American novel, to achieve the perfect orgasm, to enjoy the most blissful marriage, or to win vocational success could only be soundly addressed if I truly believed that success for the patient was not the *sine qua non* of treatment. Together the therapist and the patient should examine why success seems so necessary. It is important to know that a feeling of inner peace and self-confidence does not depend on another's opinion of you or the mark you have made in the world, that the feeling of peace is more important than any success.

Shortly after the experience with Robert, there arrived at my office for treatment a physician, Dr. Saul Epstein, and his wife. They were the parents of a seven-year-old boy, Charlie, who was also in therapy with me. Charlie was referred to me because of his unruly, belligerent, and provocative behavior at home, at school, and in the neighborhood. He was an energetic towhead with a winning smile who could flash anger in a second if opposed.

Both of Charlie's parents emphasized "proper behavior" in their son, were very controlling, and insisted on conformity at all times. They were highly embarrassed and ashamed of their only child's rebellious behavior. They believed it reflected on them as model parents who could do no wrong.

One of the axioms in my work with children and parents is that children are like dreams. Parents, like dreamers, create their children's behavior in large part, though they do not do so consciously. Like dreamers, parents often do not like what they have created. I have often observed that when a child is withdrawn, unconsciously the parents aid and abet the withdrawal. When a child rebels, the parents unconsciously sanction the rebellion. I have gone so far as to say that when a parent talks about his child, he is in many ways talking about himself. Therefore, in my work with parents, I consider descriptions of their children as presenting problems of the parents. I see their bringing children into therapy as disguised cries for help for themselves.

Just as I view chronic complaints of spouses as unconscious wishes, I view chronic complaints parents make about children as their own unconscious wishes. Just as the husband who complains his wife is cold and frigid secretly wants a cold wife who demands little tenderness or sexual fulfillment from him so does the parent who complains his child is provocative secretly want a provocative child. The child gratifies the wishes of the parent, as the child acts out feelings and wishes the parent was prohibited from experiencing as a child.

It became quite clear to me after the initial work with Charlie and his mother and father that the parents, particularly Dr. Epstein, were unconsciously enjoying and abetting Charlie's antisocial behavior. I concluded I would have to see the parents separately for weekly interviews.

During a session with Charlie's father, Saul complained about his son's provocative and rebellious behavior. I asked, "When you see your son acting this way, what images and thoughts come to your mind?"

Somewhat startled by my question, Saul proceeded to give me a long lecture on propriety and conformity, the need for controls, and the damage Charlie's behavior was inflicting on Saul personally. "It might even affect my medical practice," he complained. Then he added, "When I was a boy, my parents' rules were law. I was *always* a good boy."

"Since it was very important for you to be a good boy, it must be very shocking to you to see your only child acting like anything but a good boy." I said.

He looked thoughtful, but said no more. It took several months, during which he talked chiefly about his own childhood, before Saul said, "I want to tell you a secret: sometimes I feel like giggling when Charlie acts belligerent and provocative."

"Could you tell me more about those feelings?" I asked.

He confessed, "As a boy I would have loved to rebel, as Charlie's doing. But I always did the right thing." Then, somewhat grudgingly, he added, "I did what my parents wanted when I became a physician. I really didn't want to be a doctor, but this had been my parents' dream ever since I was a boy and I didn't want to disappoint them."

He added, as though confessing the secret of his life, "You know, I've never really enjoyed my work."

"What would you rather have done for a living?" I asked.

Embarrassed, his face flushing slightly, he said, "I've always had a secret wish to own a hot-dog stand." He added defensively, "At an amusement park or maybe near the beach at Malibu."

I smiled as I thought of this sturdy physician in his late forties, with his quiet, gracious manner, selling hot dogs. His revelation of his secret wish to defy his parents and work at something that meant play and pleasure—owning a hot-dog stand at an amusement park—triggered a fantasy I had entertained occasionally over the years. I, too, wanted to play all day and not worry about being called "a dumb boy." As the doctor spoke about the pleasure he would feel if he gave up his practice, which he had never "really enjoyed," and opened a hot-dog stand near the ocean at Malibu, I had poignant associations.

I remembered, when I was seventeen, taking a freshman composition course in college. The professor asked us to write a theme on "the happiest person I know." For my theme I chose our garbage man. I wrote about how he whistled as he worked, enjoyed the physical activity of his chores, had a sense of well-being as he performed a job on the lowest rung of the social status ladder.

The professor was so moved by my theme that she read it to the class. It obviously captured the imagination of that New York University class because when she finished reading it, the students applauded enthusiastically.

I had fantasies of becoming a garbage man and saying to my parents and all those who stood for law and order, "I want to do what comes naturally." To this day I sometimes fantasize myself helping my patients get rid of all the thoughts, feelings, and memories that are distorted and unreal—in other words, their psychic garbage.

While Saul was talking, I also recalled one of the most enjoyable summers of my life. I was nineteen, and I was selling ice cream in a low-rent housing project in New York. It was a wonderful feeling to get away from academic pursuits, to be outdoors like the garbage man, to offer people a primitive pleasure—a chance to eat ice cream.

Therefore I emphathized with Saul, who wished to work outdoors, sell hot dogs, and give up a job he hated. I knew he had enough money to do this, if he wished. He lived in a mansion in Scarsdale, an affluent suburb of New York City, his son went to a private school, and his wife owned expensive diamonds, some of which I had seen on her fingers and around her wrist during her weekly interviews.

In helping Saul cope with his secret wish to flee a vocation he disliked and take on one he enjoyed, even though it had no social status, I stood face to face with an axiom of psychoanalysis: Never tell a patient how to live. From my earliest days of practice to the present, I have strictly observed this rule. I am absolutely convinced people feel their best and function best when they decide for themselves what will make them happy.

When rules, regulations, or modes of behavior are imposed on men and women, they resent those rules, fight them, and feel like small dependent children who are expected to ape and echo their parents. I strongly believe in this axiom because as a boy I resented being instructed how to live by my parents, the Orthodox synagogue, the Boy Scouts, and the rigid Montreal schools.

But in spite of my belief in the patient's right to self-determination, a part of me wanted to tell Saul to do as he wanted, to say, "To hell with being a physician," much as I suggested that Robert say to hell with the Bar Mitzvah.

In working with Saul I had to restrain the rebel in me, the part of me that wanted to defy parental and religious authority. Many times while listening to him, I recalled selling ice cream, and I wanted him to sell hot dogs so I could enjoy myself vicariously. But just as I always have felt within me a wish to defy and question authority, I have also felt a strong desire to win the love of authority figures. This conflict was also Saul's conflict. I knew if I pushed him to rebel, he would feel guilty later on about having done so. Because I was aware of the Saul in me, I could listen to him and relate to his feelings with empathy while I refrained from offering approval or disapproval.

As we talked about his conflict over giving up the hallowed profession of medicine and opening a lowly hot-dog stand, it became clear to Saul why he was seeing me and why Charlie was having difficulties.

Charlie was expressing his father's unconscious wish to rebel against controls and provoke authorities. Charlie was an externalization of the little boy in Saul who had complied with his parents' wishes, who secretly resented them and who did not dare rebel.

Saul now reported dreams in which he saw himself in Los Angeles enjoying life, selling hot dogs at Disneyland. The dreams always ended when someone destroyed his hot-dog stand or in some other way denied him the pleasure of being a hot-dog vendor. He would wake depressed.

One day during the ninth month of our work, I said, "You have a strong wish to give up medicine and open a hot-dog stand, but you also want to be prevented from doing this."

He agreed with my interpretation. He said, "I want to be stopped from giving up medicine because by doing so I would be cursing at my mother and father, hurting them deeply, and angrily rejecting them."

I knew full well how Saul felt. He was unable to assert himself, do what he really wanted, because by doing so he was unconsciously battling his mother and father, losing their love and approval.

The ability to assert oneself comfortably, to differentiate between hostilely hurting someone and acting out of self-confidence and self-esteem, has been an everpresent concern of mine. In *Guilt: Letting Go*, I mention many times in many ways that for people to live happily and assert themselves without guilt, they have to let go of their hatred, understand it, and accept it. Know the difference between honest anger, based on reality, and neurotic rage based on fantasy. Otherwise they live plagued by uncertainty, and they never truly get pleasure out of what they do.

This was the plight of Saul. He would remain miserable in the field of medicine because he had entered it not out of his own wish but in compliance with a parental injunction. To leave his profession meant unconsciously he would be killing his parents in fantasy. In our unconscious, a fantasy seems real—the unconscious does not differentiate between reality and fantasy.

I had to do with Saul what every analyst does every day with most of his patients: help him understand why he wanted to carry on a vendetta with his parents while doing work he loathed and which he felt they had ordered him to do. I faced this in myself many times and in many ways. One of the reasons Saul and most of us find it so difficult to do as we wish without feeling guilty is that we internalize the harsh voices of our parents. We make these voices part of ourselves, constantly listen to them, act on them even though we do not like what they say. This is called the voice of conscience or, as analysts have termed it, the voices of the superego.

If Saul did not obey the commands of these voices, if he tried to break free of them, he felt like a murderous child. The voices were equivalent in his mind not only to his parents' voices but to their bodies and souls as well. This is another reason why psychoanalysis takes such a long time: it is not easy to tame the harsh voices of parents who meant the world to us in childhood. As Dr. Joseph Sandler, noted British psychoanalyst, said, we are all victims of "the voice of the ghost mother." I might add there are ghost fathers as well.

As Saul became aware how deeply he wanted to rebel against his parents and the rest of his relatives, he found himself getting into arguments with his aged parents, his wife, and his colleagues whenever he said he wanted to give up medicine, move to the West Coast, and sell hot dogs in the sunshine all year long. It came out in therapy that he remembered the exquisite pleasure of the days he had spent as a boy on the beach at Coney Island, walking along the boardwalk, eating hot dogs, gazing spellbound at the never-ending blue waves of the Atlantic.

It became apparent to me he was doing what we all do when we feel mixed emotions: we seek out people who will disagree with us because we want to hear the opposite side, much as Saul did in his dreams, where he sold hot dogs but arranged to be stopped. He was now saying to friends and colleagues, "I'd really like to give up my profession, move to California, and sell hot dogs."

They would look at him in horror and exclaim, "What a crazy idea!" A few advised, "Dream on, but forget it!"

As he reported these arguments to me, I felt his dilemma keenly. I thought of the many times I had been ambivalent about some move and had explained it to someone I knew would oppose it. While I helped Saul grapple with his ambivalence about a possible switch in careers, I thought of several times in my life when I felt as perplexed as he did.

I recalled when I was fifteen and wanted to date the sexiest, most popular girl in high school but was afraid to ask her out. I handled it just as Saul was handling his conflict: I told my sister about the girl. Without a blink of her beautiful eyes she said, "She's a tramp. You'd be a fool to date her." The more my sister opposed me, the more I could flaunt my wishes. Yet one day, when my sister ceased arguing and said, "Do what you want," I felt the ambivalence return. I started the same argument with my mother. Our inner torture and indecisiveness are temporarily relieved when we argue with someone who stands for one part of ourselves.

Because I was too frightened to admit I felt guilty about my sexual desire for this girl, I found it easier to blame my sister and mother for stopping me than to blame myself for not asking the girl for a date. I did not realize this girl was so attractive to me, and yet I suppressed my attraction to her because she reminded me of my mother and sister, stimulating intense but forbidden incestuous fantasies. This was why I needed my mother and sister to tell me not to date the desirable girl. I solved the problem by asking a less attractive girl for a date, a girl who said yes right away, a girl with whom I could go peacefully into the dark night. Because she did not arouse me too much, I felt less a sinner.

My conflict about dating the sexy, popular girl was so similar to Saul's conflict about his "date" with the hot-dog stand in California—a pleasure he coveted—that I could consistently sense the pain of his indecisiveness and his guilt over wanting to commit a forbidden act. In one session I pointed out, "You are trying to get others to stop you from switching careers. To open a hot dog stand, in your mind, would make you a despicable son, a bad father, and an irresponsible husband." (His wife thought the idea was absurd, but she had given up her hostile opposition to it.)

One day Saul arrived at a session, sat down in the chair, and promptly announced, "I had a very interesting talk with my son. I think he's changing; he doesn't seem so rebellious."

Charlie was moving along nicely in his therapy. Like most children, he progressed more rapidly than an adult. He got in touch with his feelings fairly easily, realized he had been distorting reality by believing the only way to get pleasure was to oppose those who gave orders. In my work with him—I used play therapy, since he was only seven— it became evident to me that the only time he had fun was when he opposed someone. He soon started to enjoy more acceptable ways of having fun as I permitted him to enjoy himself without censuring him.

After Saul had been in therapy a year, he told his son that he was considering giving up medicine, moving to Los Angeles, and setting up a hot-dog stand near the ocean.

To Saul's surprise, Charlie said, "Daddy, you should do what makes you happy."

I felt rewarded hearing this because it meant my work with Charlie was paying dividends. Father and son were groping with the same issues, though the son was now a little further advanced in dealing with them than was the father.

Saul used Charlie as a new conscience. On some level he knew he was getting a different response from Charlie to his wish than from his parents, wife, relatives, and friends. His wife hated the cold winters in New York, told me she thought she "might enjoy the year-round warmth of southern California." She added, "Maybe Charlie wouldn't get those miserable winter colds out there."

Saul was feeling less and less guilty about a possible move. He confessed, "The only reason for me to stay in medicine one day longer is that I feel compelled to act like an obedient boy. I'm still terrified of my parents—and that isn't a valid reason."

At the next session he said, "I think the idea of giving up medicine is realistic for me. I've been living in a nightmare." As his battle with his parents was being won, the idea of selling hot dogs became more acceptable.

One day he walked in, announced, "I've reached a decision, Dr. Strean. I am moving to Los Angeles and I am no longer going to worry about what anyone thinks. Even you."

Then, tears in his eyes, he said, "I feel you care about my happiness, not about what I do for a living. In that respect you're the kind of parent I've always wanted but never had."

I felt near tears as he put into words something I had very much wanted to say to someone at various times in my own life. My tears, I realized, were not tears of joy, because there are no tears of joy. It puzzles me that when people cry on happy occasions they believe they are shedding tears of joy. It took years for me to understand such tears are shed for the sadness we feel, not the pleasure. When a man is given a testimonial dinner and everyone praises him, he cries because he is sad about the many, many times he wanted to be treated this way and never was. Saul and I were teary on this occasion because we both silently recalled the moments we wanted to be loved for ourselves, not for our accomplishments.

Due to wise financial investments, Saul was able to open a new business in California. He probably could have moved there, lived in less lavish style, and not worked at all, but he wanted to try his hand at the kind of work he had dreamed of doing all his life.

Saul wrote me several letters over the next few years, telling me how well Charlie was doing in school. He also spoke of enjoying long hours in the sun, selling hot dogs with a smile, no doubt recalling his earlier days as a boy in Coney Island.

He said in one letter, "I feel I am at last a success after failing, in my own heart, as a physician. I am happy with myself, my family, and everyone else. I thank you more than I can say, Dr. Strean, for helping me truly enjoy my life."

I have not heard from him in the last few years. I wonder if he has given up selling hot dogs and found some other pursuit. He always loved reading the classics—perhaps he is teaching English literature in some university or college.

I do not think I would have been able to help Saul if I hadn't spent many years on the couch dealing with a similar conflict. It took a long time for me to feel free to do as I wished, because I felt I had to submit to my parents like an obedient child rather than tell them what I thought.

While working with Saul, I remembered a poignant episode during my own analysis. One Christmas I went south with my wife and two sons. I did not particularly enjoy the vacation because I felt I was playing hooky from my teacher-analyst, defying him as I wanted to defy my parents, rabbis, and other figures of authority. I was "playing" while my analyst was working; I felt I should have been attending my analytic session.

Only after I gave up my hatred toward those I felt made me submit was I able to help others do the same thing. I helped Saul become free enough to make up his own mind. He became a success when he refused to be chained to a profession that brought him not one whit of pleasure.

My work with Saul helped me realize once again the importance of a remark Freud once made: "No psychoanalyst goes further than his own complexes and internal resistances permit." In other words, a psychoanalyst can help his patient go only as far as he himself has traveled in knowing himself.

6

THE PATIENT AS CONSULTANT
The Boy Who Prescribed
His Own Treatment

During the late 1950s when I was in the middle of my psychoanalytic training, I found myself in a constant state of confusion. While I studied classical psychoanalysis, my instructors and many writers of psychoanalytic literature were discussing and recommending departures from classical psychoanalytic technique.

Family therapy was being introduced, group therapy was becoming popular, and long-term treatment, the cornerstone of psychoanalysis, was being questioned. Short-term treatment, known as crisis intervention, and a host of other new modalities were being championed. In some of these new therapies, the analyst even shared aspects of his own life with the patient in order to facilitate a working alliance between himself and the patient.

Sometimes I would go to class, believe I had at last incorporated a dimension of mainstream psychoanalytic theory into my professional ego, only to find two days later that a supervisor, teacher, or writer was questioning something I regarded as gospel.

I began to feel what every learner feels—ambivalence toward my teachers and anger at the school I attended. I even wondered from time to time whether psychoanalysis was the right profession for me. During this period I experimented with behavior modification, a type of treatment in which the therapist avoids interpretations and offers the patient advice instead.

These departures from traditional therapy were justified, I rationalized in those days, if they allowed an analyst to help a patient. (I now believe that these procedures are often used to help the analyst cope with his own anxieties, uncertainties, and frustrations.)

Whenever I have found myself departing from classical Freudian analysis, or have observed such a departure in students, supervisees, or colleagues, inevitably I discover the departure serves me or the other therapist more than it helps the patient. Unfortunately, few analysts, including myself, recognize this while they are using the departure.

During the late 1950s I heard and read about many new treatment procedures, but I found the new techniques increasingly difficult to master. I spent many hours attempting to solve this dilemma. One of the ideas that evolved from my study of the new procedures was a wish to see to what extent a patient could prescribe his own treatment and what results could be achieved through this kind of therapy.

It seems clear to me now that I was fed up with professional consultants and angry at the conflicting advice I received. As a result, I decided perhaps the patient knows best. Though I now regard this period in my life as an attempt to cope with some developmental conflicts in myself, I still believe some patients, some of the time, know better than anyone else what they need from their analyst, just as many children know better than anyone else what they need from their parents.

Jerry Murphy was a fourteen-year-old boy referred to me by school officials. I was told he had failed several subjects, was exceedingly withdrawn at home and at school, took part in virtually no extracurricular activities, and could not read. His persistent negativism and social isolation were apparent in all of his relationships. This was a boy who "wanted nothin' from nobody."

Jerry was the only child of a severely depressed mother who had been in a mental hospital several times for short stays. His father, a mechanic, was a passive, withdrawn man who showed little emotional spontaneity with either his family or strangers.

Several other therapists had tried to help Jerry with his learning problems and his inability to relate to other people. Jerry had so frustrated the therapists that all attempts at treatment had ended prematurely: Jerry either quit or appeared so unmotivated and uncommunicative that the therapist gave up.

Perhaps because I, too, was conflicted at the time, I found Jerry intriguing. I was struggling to learn more about psychoanalysis, and I resented the new approaches. Like Jerry, I distrusted my teachers and felt somewhat withdrawn. I could easily empathize with my young patient's anger at and disillusionment with authority.

His provocative negativism and his withdrawal from the mainstream of life were quite similar to my own negativism toward my studies and my withdrawal from mainstream psychoanalysis. Just as Jerry had difficulty adapting to the educational requirements of his school, I was having difficulties adapting to the educational requirements of the institute I attended.

Jerry was tall for his fourteen years—five feet seven inches. He was very thin and had a pale but rather appealing face. He never smiled, was clearly depressed. His dark brown eyes looked straight into mine as he spoke. He dressed carelessly, and his brown hair looked uncombed.

In his first interview he told me his four previous therapists had not helped him at all. He also implied they were similar to his parents—uncaring, insensitive, and emotionally unavailable.

I said, "I guess you feel I will probably fail you, too. Why should I be any different from anyone else?"

He nodded in agreement, then said, "I don't think teachers or shrinks can help me." He shrugged. "Maybe they can help other people. I'm not saying they can't."

As he told me of shrinks not helping him but perhaps able to help others, I felt a strong kinship with Jerry. At the time I thought many of my fellow students at the institute were mastering psychoanalysis when I was failing to do so. Just as Jerry was at war with his mentors, so was I.

Because of my own hostility, and also partly because I wanted some magical solution to my conflicts in which I could be master instead of frustrated student, I used a therapeutic approach with Jerry that tended to gratify some of my wishes.

I told him frankly, "I want to keep you in treatment, but you have defeated every therapist in the past, so it's a safe bet the same thing will happen to me. What should I do?"

He responded, "I can tell you are the same as the other guys, but I'll come back here for another try."

After that he said not a word for fifteen minutes. During the silence I realized Jerry expected me to try to force him to talk, much as his teachers were trying to force him to learn. I knew I had to respect his wish to withdraw because I was in a withdrawn mood myself. I could also see some positive aspects in his withdrawal.

But I began to find the silence unbearable, so I said, "You remind me of a very famous man—Gandhi, the spiritual leader of India."

"I never heard of him," Jerry said.

"He accomplished a great deal by saying nothing," I explained. Then I asked, "Can you teach me to become like the Gandhi you are?"

Jerry, a wise fourteen-year-old, countered, "You're just trying to get me to keep coming here."

"You're right," I admitted. "I want you to come here because I feel I can learn from you. I'm very much interested in someone who has successfully defeated so many therapists."

Jerry said, somewhat petulantly, "You talk too much. You're long-winded."

"You're probably right," I granted.

Then he said grudgingly, "I might try to teach you to be quiet. If you were quiet, I might consider coming back to see you."

As he left the office, Jerry warned, "You have to promise to say nothing next time. I'll be the boss."

I was determined to keep my promise to Jerry. I felt the usual methods of treating a child would not work with him. Despite his arrogance, grandiosity, and air of omnipotence, I thought his prescription for treatment had some merit.

Jerry returned for several interviews. Both of us remained silent, merely looking at each other every so often with no exchange except hello and good-bye. But suddenly in the middle of the sixth session, Jerry broke the silence. "I'm quitting!" he announced. "I don't like it here. Nothing is happening. You're no better than the other guys."

I said what I felt: "Jerry, I must be doing something wrong. Where am I making mistakes? What can I do to make coming here worthwhile for you?"

He said, "I don't want to teach you anything. I'm getting nothing out of it."

Again I asked quietly but firmly, "What should I do?"

Jerry retreated into silence, but this time he was active instead of passive. He started to draw on paper with a pen he took from his pocket. He sketched complicated electrical circuits, imagined how he would burn down my office. He said with pride, "I could set your office on fire, burn up your books and you. You're a lousy therapist and these books don't help anybody."

At least he was showing emotion, I thought, and at the same time demonstrating his skill in drawing and his knowledge of electricity. As he stood up to leave—I really thought this time he would depart permanently—I said, relating more to my own needs than his, "Maybe you can teach me something about electricity."

He walked out the door with the comment, spoken almost sagely, "You've got a lot to learn. I'll think about coming back and showing you."

Jerry returned for two more silent sessions. Then, without encouragement from me, he drew several more electrical circuit plans which he then explained, granting my wish to know more about electricity. Electricity became the sole subject of communication for several more sessions, with Jerry as teacher, I as pupil.

Then once again his negative attitude asserted itself. He said wearily, "I'm tired of being the big shot. It's about time you did something for me."

"What do you think I should do?"

"Coming to your office is just like going to school," he said. "It's plain dull; nothing happens. The only difference is that here I can work on my electricity once in a while."

At this point I had an idea I thought might work. I said, "I realize you want me to do something for you. Maybe I can find you an electrical school."

"There's no such thing," he said contemptuously. "You couldn't do anything about it anyway, even if there was."

Again I asked, "What *should* I do?"

Jerry advised, "Don't get so excited. Do less talking. And give with more action."

All right, I thought, I will try to "give with more action." I set about finding a school that taught electricity. Though it took me several weeks to locate one, Jerry was tolerant of my slowness. He frequently remarked as I reported I was still searching, "Take your time. It's not that important."

Finally I found a vocational school that specialized in electricity. Jerry visited it and became very enthusiastic. He was accepted by the school, began to develop relationships with other students, and started to read and earn high marks.

He continued seeing me to report on his activities. After one and a half years of twice-a-week treatment, he suggested one day, "I think this case should be closed. I'm doing all right now."

He handed me an essay he had written: "A Closing Summary on Herb Strean." In it he both criticized and praised me, giving a colorful picture of the treatment process. He was clear about my anxiety at times and how much I identified with him. He showed awareness of many of my motives. Jerry was far from a retarded or stupid boy—primarily an angry one. Justifiably so, in terms of his childhood with a mentally ill mother and a father who paid no attention to him.

My unusual therapeutic work with Jerry focused on two points: the impact of the analytic relationship on him and its effect on me. Jerry gained self-assurance and motivation and, as time went on, involved himself more in understanding himself. Perhaps the main reason for his increased involvement was that at first there was no therapy to resist. I, the therapist, was the patient in many ways. I was the learner, and Jerry was the therapist and teacher. When Jerry tried to withdraw from me, he received a response different from that of his previous therapists: I neither protested nor supported his withdrawal; I simply compared him favorably with Gandhi.

Later, as I cast off my professional cloak, Jerry was able to loosen some of his defenses. When I showed I could take advice from him, he began asking for something from me. Then as he saw I appeared relatively unthreatened as a student and learner, he slowly identified with me, started to show interest in school. In brief, he became more aware of himself as a human being; he had never felt human with his very disturbed parents.

I believe the patient's identification with the analyst is one of the most therapeutic factors in all psychotherapy, but it is rarely given the prominence it deserves. Just as all children identify with their parents, for better or worse, all patients identify with their analysts. This identification is made in many ways, on many levels. The patient may absorb the therapist's way of thinking or speaking, may even adopt his mannerisms. As a supervisor, after I talked to a student for a few minutes I knew with whom he was in analysis, because he had adopted some characteristic of his analyst. When I was a student, a popular analyst had a Boston accent, and a number of his patients revealed themselves when they began to speak with a Boston accent.

Psychoanalysis, which has features of both learning, as in school, and child-rearing, as at home, makes the analyst, whether he wants to be or not, a role model for the patient. Overtly and covertly, directly and indirectly, the analyst is always presenting himself as a model for identification. All of us hunger for a parental figure, a teacher, to show us the way. Jerry, when he could identify with someone who did not threaten him, could begin to involve himself in a more intimate, cooperative relationship.

I believe analysts are often reluctant to admit they are role models because they strongly believe they are neutral observers who never show their real values. Yet, even as the analyst spends most of his time quietly listening, he puts a value on the limits of the time a patient talks. When an analyst says, after forty-five or fifty minutes of hearing the patient, "We have to stop," he means, "I value the notion of showing you that you can't have everything," meaning all of his time.

I strongly believe the analyst is a model for identification; therefore I feel the analyst must be as mature and self-aware as possible. As I have stated repeatedly, borrowing from Freud, an analyst can help a patient grow emotionally only as much as the analyst has grown emotionally.

While the issue of a patient's identification with the analyst has been minimally written about in analytic literature, even more neglected are descriptions and examinations of the analyst's identification with the patient. I believe it is necessary for the analyst emotionally to step into the shoes of a patient in order to understand what he feels, to be empathic with the patient's conflicts, and to say, in one way or another, "I've been there, too." Therapists may overidentify or underidentify with a patient. It takes constant vigilance and self-discipline to feel within oneself a patient's loves and hates without losing the analytic stance.

In hindsight I can see that I overidentified with Jerry. The relationship, while very helpful to him, was a bit too gratifying for me. I received too much vicarious pleasure from defying authority with him. Jerry's refusal to read and take part in school activities was similar to some of my reactions to supervisors and my exasperation with parts of the psychoanalytic literature.

While the vicarious pleasure I derived from identifying with Jerry's hostility was not harmful to him, perhaps even helped him, I now believe I could have reached him without using such dramatic intervention. Had I shown Jerry greater compassion, more understanding of his resentments and his desire to defeat me, related to his fear of his inadequate parents, I probably could have helped him more. I took the risk of helping him become too much of a rebel without a cause.

Yet Jerry knew I empathized with his deep fear and distrust of everyone. He also knew I was trying my best to avoid acting like an authoritarian therapist. But I have to acknowledge our sessions were perhaps more therapeutic for me than for him. As I saw Jerry lessen his fight with authorities, become a more social human being, the same things started to happen to me: I became a less rebellious analytic student.

Few analysts have talked or written about what they have learned from their patients. I know of only two who have done so: Dr. Harold Searles and Dr. Reuben Fine. I believe Searles goes a bit too far when he talks of patients "curing" their analysts. Patients may help an analyst think more clearly about a certain conflict, but this is not cure. I do think that whether they acknowledge it or not, analysts often unconsciously emulate the means of coping used by patients. I also believe that an analyst—if he truly thinks there are dimensions of life and of analytic work he can learn from a patient—can help a patient like Jerry who cannot tolerate, at least at the start of treatment, being a passive recipient of the therapist's wisdom.

Since my experience with Jerry, I have always learned something new about life or about psychoanalysis from my patients. To some extent all my patients are consultants. I have also discovered that the only way to reach very negative, stubborn, controlling individuals is to let them take control as I follow. It is seldom easy to abdicate one's authority, but with certain patients it is necessary to do so for a while at the beginning of treatment.

About a year after I finished working with Jerry, I was sought for consultation by the father of a boy I was treating. Max David was forty-five years old; he was not interested in treatment for himself but wanted to talk about his dissatisfaction with the way I was treating his twelve-year-old son, Morton.

Morton was a frightened boy, deathly afraid of the dark. He had strong feelings of inferiority, could not tolerate competition or aggression, and was extremely passive and overly compliant. Both he and his mother had been in treatment with me for six months when Mr. David came in and objected to his son's increasing assertiveness. He had called me on the phone to announce, "I'm coming down to bawl you out. You don't know what you're doing."

He arrived ten minutes late for his appointment. When he walked in, he marched to my chair, the therapist's seat, sat down defiantly. "I'm going to tell you a thing or two," he said. "I know all about this psychology stuff. There are many things wrong with the way you run your business." He, by the way, was a certified public accountant who earned a respectable living.

I replied, "I'm glad to learn about my mistakes."

He declared angrily, "My son has to be dealt with very firmly or else he can't be kept in line." He added, "Permissiveness is a lot of hokum. Nobody should be mollycoddled. You're doing that to him."

"Tell me how you think I should treat your son," I said.

Mr. David replied, "You have to set firm limits and controls. Don't be so indulgent."

At the end of the interview I thanked him and said it would be helpful to me to see him again. We set the hour for a second interview, and this time he arrived promptly. He again sat in my chair and proceeded to vilify and condemn me and my profession. "Why don't you get out of this field and learn how to make real money?" he barked.

I responded, "Maybe that's a good idea."

In succeeding interviews he continued to give advice on people in general and his son in particular. But during the sixth session, Mr. David seemed subdued. As soon as he arrived, he told me, "You can have your seat back," and he took the patient's chair.

Then he said, "I thank you for taking all my guff. You've been doing the right thing."

"What do you mean?" I asked.

He explained, "A big change has come over my son. I started to listen to him as you listen to me. It works like magic. I think I understand the boy for the first time."

Mr. David consented to join a fathers' group I conducted at that time, saying, "Maybe I can learn from and teach the other fathers."

Had I not been through the experience with Jerry, where I learned the therapeutic benefits of abdicating some of my authority and letting the patient be the boss, I could not have helped a man like Mr. David. He reminded me very much of my own father—authoritarian, dominating, seemingly self-assured—just as Mr. David's son Morton reminded me very much of myself—frightened of his father, competitive with and aggressive toward him.

For a long time, when I worked with parents like Mr. David, I had tended to become somewhat authoritarian with them. Not realizing I was working out my feelings of revenge toward my father, trying to get him to realize the vulnerability I had felt as a child.

Much of my battle with my father was unconscious, and the authoritarian approach I had used with patients who reminded me of my father was also unconscious. It took a while to resolve my revengeful feelings toward father figures. My capacity to empathize with fear in the authoritarian father himself was a long time coming. To this day, when I am in the company of an angry, belligerent, authoritarian man, either in or out of psychoanalysis, I still have a tendency to want to engage in a power struggle, to embarrass or humiliate the other man as my father did to me. I know that if I had not faced these hidden feelings in analysis, I could not have helped men like Mr. David.

My experience with patients like Jerry and Mr. David have affirmed for me that the most arrogant and dominating patients are often the most frightened. If I keep that in mind, I do not get into power struggles, as I was tempted to do in the past with my father and other father figures. I believe every analyst at times should be able to say directly or indirectly to all of his patients what I could say to Jerry and Mr. David: "You teach me. I'm ready to learn."

7

THE WOMAN WHO WANTED TO DEVOUR ME
Analyzing a Psychotic Patient

One day I received a phone call from a woman who said she was an elementary school teacher. She explained she had heard me speak at meetings, read some of my books and articles, and wanted a consultation about a child in her classroom.

I have always enjoyed consultations with other professionals. They give me an opportunity to apply psychoanalytic understanding to other fields and to enrich my own understanding through insights from other disciplines.

When I asked this woman, who said her name was Judith Simon, to come for a consultation, I did not realize she would end up on my couch four times a week for several years.

At the scheduled hour, into my office walked a woman in her middle forties, with light brown hair and pale blue eyes. She was plain-looking, simply dressed. As she talked, I sensed she was extremely articulate, sensitive, and intelligent. She explained she was consulting me about an eight-year-old boy in her class who could not respond to discipline; he threw violent temper tantrums when anyone gave him an instruction.

Over the years I have held as an axiom that when anyone, but particularly a parent or a teacher, talks about a child, he is talking about himself. I wondered how Judith expressed her severe anger, how she controlled her impulses.

"What do you find difficult in coping with this boy?" I asked.

She answered, "Nothing bothers me about the child. It's the principal of the school I can't stand. He told this boy I was poisoning his mind." She added, "This principal, Mr. McConnell, is also spreading malicious rumors about me to all my pupils and their parents, as well as my colleagues." She fell silent for a few moments, then said, "I'm really consulting you because my life is in danger. I believe Mr. McConnell is out to destroy me and my reputation."

I felt I was dealing with a schizophrenic woman. She confirmed this diagnosis when she confided that from time to time in her life she had met other people like Mr. McConnell. "Five years ago, one of my colleagues tried to poison my soup while we were eating in the school cafeteria," she said. "My colleague's attempt to kill me upset me so much I had to go into the hospital to recover."

She then reported she had been in and out of mental hospitals since the age of nineteen. She said she suffered from delusions and hallucinations at times, had made at least a dozen suicide attempts. I also found out in this interview, which was to have been a consultation about a pupil, that she was the "victim" of a "miserable" marriage. She said, "My husband criticized me all the time and set my two children against me." She had a son fifteen and a daughter seventeen.

I had learned many years before that when any patient, particularly one who is psychotic, departs from reality in that he believes he is going to be poisoned or killed, the therapist cannot or should not try to talk the patient out of a distorted belief but simply listen with a sympathetic ear.

So I listened and learned more from Judith about her life, including her childhood. She said her mother and father never wanted her. They "hated" her and favored her older brother, discriminating against her in every way.

I brought her back to her problem with the boy in her class: "I realize you are suffering from what goes on in school, and I'd like to discuss it further with you," meaning a few consultations. But then I heard from her what would become a characteristic verbal pattern.

She said almost entreatingly, "Can I see you every day, seven days a week, until we get to the bottom of all this?"

I realized I could not tell her I liked to relax on weekends and her demands were rather excessive. Instead, I suggested she come to my office as many times a week as our mutual schedules would permit. She responded, "I'm disappointed you can't see me every day, but I'll try my best to accept it." Traveling to my office involved coming to the city from her home in Long Island, a trip of well over an hour each way.

As I listened to Judith during that initial consultation, I was associating silently to the issue of psychoanalysts working with schizophrenic patients. It has been, and still is, a very controversial question for several reasons. Many analysts do not conduct therapy with psychotic patients in their offices, probably in part because of Freud's attitude toward psychoanalytic work with such patients.

Freud constantly pointed out that the difference between the so-called normal person and the psychotic was only a matter of degree. He also noted that what the so-called normal person dreams at night, the psychotic thinks or acts out during the day. Despite this point of view, Freud was quite pessimistic about psychoanalysis helping schizophrenic and other psychotic patients.

Like many clinicians, Freud justified his own personal discomfort with such patients in theoretical terms. He claimed the psychotic patient is much too narcissistic to form a working relationship with the analyst, and hence psychoanalysis is not an appropriate means of treatment. This point of view is still shared by many psychoanalysts, though a number sharply disagree. Dr. Harry Stack Sullivan, Dr. John Frosch, Dr. Silvano Arieti, Dr. Harold Searles, and Dr. John Rosen have reported effective results using the psychoanalytic method with psychotic patients.

I believe psychoanalysis can work with the psychotic patient if the analyst believes it can—if he does not feel helpless and angry because he is uncomfortable with the hallucinations, delusions, and paranoia of the patient. The analyst, in other words, must not be afraid or feel hopeless; he must believe he can help. This is the *sine qua non* of the treatment of psychosis.

I also believe many schizophrenic patients are given shock therapy, drug therapy, and forms of treatment other than psychotherapy because the practitioners who use these methods are terrified by the psychotic patient's rages, helplessness, infantile behavior, and other qualities the therapist cannot tolerate in himself.

Whether an analyst can work with a psychotic patient has a great deal to do with his own life story and his experiences with mental illness, either in his family or in his patients. My comfort in working with schizophrenic patients arose out of my past. When I took oral examinations for my doctoral degree at Columbia University, the professor asked me to describe a schizophrenic patient, a hysterical patient, a "paranoid" or "narcissistic-disorder" patient as they appeared to me.

I evidently answered these questions to his satisfaction, because when the examination was over the professor said, "I assume you made your descriptions of these patients seem so alive because you worked with them in therapy."

I laughed. "Not really," I admitted. "When you asked me about schizophrenia, I thought of an aunt. When you asked about a narcissistic character disorder, I thought of an uncle. When you asked about hysteria, I thought of my mother. When you asked about paranoia, I thought of my father."

Though I have always been something of a showman, I did not anticipate the roar of laughter from this rather austere professor. The truth was that as a child and adolescent I had to adapt continually to mental illness of one sort or another among relatives, though at the time I did not know it was mental illness. It was not until I went to college that I realized my aunt was psychotic and most of my close relatives were coping with some degree of serious emotional illness.

My capacity to empathize with and adapt to severe mental disturbances was related to my eagerness to sustain relationships with my mother and father, whom I needed in order to survive. While I developed many ways, some maladaptive, to handle my relatives' *meshugas* (in Yiddish, "craziness"), nonetheless I believe my unwavering quest to get along with them has been transmitted into my work with very disturbed patients, making it possible for me to accept them.

Judith reminded me of both my mother and my aunt, and during her treatment I frequently thought my mother or my aunt could be lying there on that couch as I listened to Judith's outbursts.

After she started treatment, Judith's obsession about the school principal became more and more dramatic. She kept saying Mr. McConnell wanted to make her a "victim." He was "poisoning" the minds of her pupils and colleagues, turning them against her.

I asked, "Why is he singling you out and trying to make you suffer?"

She replied, "He's the kind of man who always wanted me to suffer. He's a lot like my father, who's a prominent attorney and always persecuting people, trying to put them in prison. Mr. McConnell is like my brother, too; he followed in my father's footsteps and is a partner in his law firm."

She called the principal, her father, and her brother "cruel men" and said they were out to exploit her "vulnerability." All three she described as "tall, big, competent, the kind of men who want to rape your mind and destroy your strength." Judith sometimes talked in a literary way.

I knew she suffered strong delusions of persecution when she told me she was convinced that the principal, like her brother and father, wanted to render her so weak mentally she would have to be hospitalized once more. She then related her experiences in the mental hospitals where she'd been a patient off and on since the age of nineteen. As I listened, I totalled the number of hospitals as five; she'd stayed in one for a year.

I asked what had caused her at nineteen to need hospitalization.

She said, "I was forced to leave college because the professors were out to weaken my mind, just as my husband wanted to destroy me later in life, and my brother and father earlier."

She expressed fear the principal would succeed in forcing her back into a mental hospital where she would again be the victim of psychiatrists. She called them "cruel men, ready to hit you over the head and call it shock therapy," which she had endured, "or make you swallow poison and call it some kind of tranquilizer."

As Judith talked of being poisoned, hit over the head, destroyed in some fashion, she reminded me of my paranoid Aunt Mathilde, who also had been in mental hospitals. Early in childhood and throughout adolescence I learned to adapt to Aunt Mathilde as she told me again and again how certain people were out to get her. Waiters and waitresses were trying to poison her soup, she insisted. Friends and relatives were trying to steal money from her.

Because I knew Aunt Mathilde loved me, I could listen to her delusions of persecution as if she were a child playing games; I never took her too seriously. Other members of my family felt frightened of her, intimidated by her, but somehow she took to me early on. As I look back, I can see how she helped me remain empathic, even loving, toward severely disturbed people, particularly those who suffer from paranoia.

Having undergone the experience of Aunt Mathilde, it did not surprise me when, early in psychoanalytic training, I read in Freud's works that the paranoid person has deep wishes to love and be loved but is afraid to acknowledge them. Feeling rejected by his mother and father, the person says in sour-grapes fashion, "I do not love, I hate." Then, finding his own hatred unacceptable, he projects it on others, claiming, "*You* hate *me.*"

As a child, I realized intuitively that everything Aunt Mathilde accused others of wanting to do, *she* wanted to do—poison, steal, kill. As an adult and a therapist, I realized that Judith was filled with rage at her father, her brother, and the principal—and she projected her rage onto them. By claiming the other person hates him, the paranoid person believes he frees himself of an intolerable hatred. Senator Joseph McCarthy, for example, accused people of participating in a Communist conspiracy, thus renouncing his own wish to conspire against and to hate others. Paranoia is a matter of degree, for there is a certain amount of suspiciousness and hatred in all of us (it serves us well when we want to protect ourselves against real enemies). In the paranoid person this suspicion is out of hand.

Another thing I learned from Aunt Mathilde is that you never question a paranoid person's distortions. If you do, you only make the person angrier, more aggravated. As a child, I wanted Aunt Mathilde's love, and so I did not contradict her. As a result, she loved me more than the others, who treated her like a "crazy" person and said her delusions were ridiculous.

I knew that at some point in Judith's treatment she would regard me as a persecutor. But now, as I listened to her delusions of persecution without question or censure, she related to me much as my Aunt Mathilde did. Judith told me, after a month of treatment, "You are the kindest man I have ever met. You really listen to me. You are very non-judgmental."

She contrasted me with previous analysts, psychiatrists in hospitals, and other therapists who "tried to talk me out of my delusions, as they put it." She sensed I was trying to understand and help her. But soon her warmth and admiration became a difficult problem for me. She wanted to cling to me, did not wish to end her therapeutic hour, called me many times between sessions. She even found out where I lived, phoned me at home to say, "I can't live without you."

Judith's intense and persistent infantile demands were now surfacing and for several reasons were difficult to cope with. For one, I knew that if in any way I tried to persuade her to call less frequently or curtail her demands for more of my time, I would frustrate her, she would become angrier, and this would increase her paranoia. I also knew from her experiences with previous analysts that to gratify her wishes would make her want more and more of my attention, and would not help her in the long run.

For a second reason, a demanding woman brings out in me resentments I held toward my mother, who wanted a lot from me but was able to give me little in return. I felt this same resentment toward Judith as she badgered me with requests for more time. As a child, I had found it hard to say no to my mother, who threw temper tantrums if I did not fulfill her requests pronto.

It was a tough dilemma, but I knew that, like a baby, Judith needed to be weaned, emotionally speaking. I also knew if I tried to wean her abruptly or in anger, I would turn her into a raging baby.

When I could in my mind separate Judith from my mother and separate the angry boy in me from the mature analyst, I could start to do for Judith what previous helping professionals could not—provide her with necessary limits, realize she was very angry, and help her feel and express the anger without threatening punishment. This is what every infant who is weaned and toilet-trained needs—a parent who can live through the child's frustrated anger and temper tantrums.

During the third month of Judith's treatment, I told her it would be much more helpful for our work if she could tell me directly everything she felt, refrain from describing it during phone calls between sessions. I also told her it would be helpful for our work if she could end the sessions when I said, "Our time is up," instead of insisting on staying, holding up other patients.

Though I felt like a conscientious parent as I said this, she responded as if I were an ogre. She snapped, "You're a selfish, cruel therapist. You don't give a damn about me. If you really cared, you'd be on call all the time, because I'm a bruised person. But you obviously don't care."

She added, "You are just like my brother, my father, and the principal—but more so. You're an egocentric narcissist. You're only here to enhance yourself."

I let her go on—what was there to say? She needed to release her childhood anger at obviously uncaring parents. In one session she bellowed, "You should be reported to all professional associations for being a total incompetent. You deserve to be murdered!"

Judith's rages and rantings were powerful, which I expected, and, as I had predicted, I became part of her paranoid system. She accused me of being a "killer," said she did not know how someone like me could be a therapist, since I was obviously "murderous, sadistic, ignorant, and stupid." She charged me with not having graduated from college, accused me of falsifying my diploma.

A part of me felt like asking Judith why, if I were so incompetent, she did not seek another therapist. I realized all too soon that she was trying to provoke me into throwing her out. She wanted to prove to herself that every helping professional was indeed a persecutor and prosecutor (like her hated father).

While experiencing me as excessively sadistic, Judith recalled the sadism of her mother and father, who forced her to stay in her room for hours at a time because of minor infractions such as coming home twenty minutes late. They also insisted she was faking when she was really ill. They would contrast her "bad behavior" to that of her godlike brother, obviously the favored one.

Judith's anguish as a child was something I could easily identify with. Perhaps more than any other patient with whom I have worked in my professional life, which at this writing spans over thirty years, Judith had a profound therapeutic effect on me. I began to realize, more than I ever had before, how beneath my mother's sadism hid a frightened woman like Judith, one who felt vulnerable and weak, afraid to love a boy. As I worked with Judith, I started to feel more warmly toward my mother. I saw that underneath her rage lay a very distressed woman.

As this occurred to me, Judith sensed a more benign attitude on my part, and her raving began to diminish. Whenever the analyst becomes the object of a patient's distortions, usually the patient begins to function better on the outside. This happened to Judith. Her teaching became more professional and objective, she was more relaxed with her own children and friends. She felt less vitriolic toward her former husband, whom she had left three years before the analysis began.

As Judith's rage toward me diminished, she began to tell me over and over what she most appreciated about me: I never wanted to punish or criticize her. She said, "I feel less and less crazy, both when I'm with you and when I'm outside."

She pointed out something that was to arise many times: her previous analysts and other therapists had become furious at her, felt helpless when she was out of control. This made her experience her therapeutic helpers as if they were the parents who had frequently punished her.

She said to me, "Your even-tempered attitude is more important to me than anything else. I'm beginning to love you."

Judith's way of relating to me was no different from any other patients—except more so, including her sexual desires. Her sexual fantasies were very intense and infantile. She daydreamed of having me in bed with her twenty-four hours a day, seven days a week, holding her, hugging her, my penis inside her. Frequently she wanted to devour me, fantasying this again and again. She was clearly trying to make me not into a lover but into a symbiotic mother who would merge with her.

As I pointed out earlier, many male analysts, including myself, have felt all too flattered when a woman patient said she wanted them inside her all the time. It is a blow to our male narcissism to realize this expresses a wish for an all-giving mother and an all-nurturing breast, not for a handsome, virile man. Unless analysts and patients understand this basic need, the one that precedes all others in our early lives, the therapy is incomplete.

I could identify with Judith's sexual fantasies, since I, too, had spent many of my own analytic sessions wanting to merge with my male analyst, whom at times I fantasized as a mother. I could help Judith talk about her wish for a good mother, her rage at her own mother for being unavailable. I could also help her understand she frequently fell physically ill because only through illness could she receive the feeling of being mothered, usually by male doctors.

Judith's severe need to merge indicated she experienced her mother as exceptionally unable to give tenderness, love, and empathy. She wrote me one day: "I've always known I am haunted by a terror that is primitive and wordless and known to me alone. Your metaphor of a baby nursing at the breast of a remote, self-absorbed, unrelated mother took my breath away, literally. I felt about my mother that I would be afraid to nurse at her breast because I could choke to death and she wouldn't even notice. I was nursed for three days, she told me, and then she caught pneumonia and that put an end to the nursing.

"Is it possible I am reacting to some very early experience in my infancy, and my response to anything that frightens me is a paradigm for my lifelong interaction with my mother? I do remember looking at baby pictures and noticing my mother was always staring into the camera and the baby she was holding—either my brother or me—looked like an ornament she was wearing, not a person she was holding. Later, when my mother kissed my children, she'd touch them stiffly, put her face near theirs but kiss the air, not their cheeks. She was afraid of the touch.

"My terror is real and it's been with me as long as I can remember. So far as I'm concerned, on a gut and thinking level, being together is the only solution, the only state of being that offers protection to my sense of impending annihilation, whether I'm with another person or by myself. Whether I'm sick or well, big or little. So now you and I are speaking the same language." This was Judith addressing me.

I felt proud of her for being able to accept a feeling few of us are able to admit—our inability to separate ourselves emotionally from a mother who did not know how to help us do so. Dr. Margaret Mahler spent her entire professional life trying to show that this emotional separation is crucial to a mature adult life.

When one person shows some trust in another, as Judith was starting to trust me, he is ready to move into more intimate relationships. In her relationships with me and with others, Judith began to feel more sexual and less anxious about her sexual fantasies. Toward the end of her second year of treatment, she started to date men, began to think of me more as a sexual man than as a mother. But because she had such poor self-image as a girl, then as a woman, once again she began to resent me and the men in her life. She started up the old angry verbal barrages. "You think you're such a big shot because you've got something between your legs," she would say. "You remind me of my brother and father, both male chauvinists."

She talked about situations, both in her family and at school, where she had been clearly discriminated against because she was a girl. My own feelings of guilt toward my sister emerged as I thought of the times I had it better than she. Earlier in my career I had a tendency to act out my guilt toward my sister when women patients talked about their feelings of low self-esteem compared to mine. In some ways I felt I had to build up their self-esteem rather than help them unravel their distortions. But by the time I worked with Judith in the late 1970s, when I had more experience, I could monitor the residue of guilt in myself, listen empathically to her resentment at being a woman.

As I heard her fantasies of wanting a penis and wishing to be a man, I was able to help her by doing what I had learned many women in analysis need: finding out why she devalued her vagina. Unless the analyst does this, a woman may continue wanting a penis for the rest of her life. If she is unable to give up her wish to be a man, nothing much will happen in the analysis or in her life.

Judith shared many of her fantasies about her vagina. It was "a destroyed penis." In her mind, her vagina was a large wound from which blood issued each month. This is a common enough distortion among women, but with Judith it appeared pervasive and intense. She also had fantasies of being castrated by her mother, whom she described throughout most of the analysis as "cold and heartless."

The more I worked with Judith the more she became like any other patient. I was increasingly certain that psychosis can and does exist in all of us to some degree. We all depart from reality when life seems frightening or provokes deep anxiety. When our anger is acute, we need to justify it by finding enemies where they do not exist. Or if they do exist, we need to keep the battles going.

I also believe, particularly after my work with Judith, that many of the methods used in the treatment of psychotic patients do more to assuage the professional's feelings of helplessness and anger (and wish to punish) than to help the patient. It is easier for many therapists to verbally "hit somebody over the head" with shock treatment than to listen to the patient's murderous fantasies, hallucinations, delusions, and expressions of paranoia.

I sometimes wondered if I would be treating Judith for the rest of my life. Would I "cure" her? I asked myself. I thought about all the discussion in analytic papers about what "cure" means. I think it's a misleading word to use about psychoanalysis. "Cure" is a medical word that applies to physical illness. An analyst's patients are not "cured." They are helped to understand their lives better, to know that the conflicts they have faced will continue to exist but that they are now capable of handling them emotionally, not letting them rule their lives. They are no longer victims of their inner desires; they understand these desires and can control them or give in to them at will in such a way that the desires do not harm them or others.

As I carefully examined my work with Judith, I could say with deep conviction, "The psychotic patient is normal— only more so." By that I mean he or she has the same wishes, the same angers, the same loves as all mortals. But these patients feel their anger more keenly, their dependency more acutely, and because fear stems from deep anguish and desperation, it leads to a state of greater vulnerability and regression.

But human the schizophrenic is, first and foremost. Unless we consider him a human being, we cannot treat him psychoanalytically. But if we see him as "more human than otherwise," as Dr. Sullivan says, we can help him out of the depths of his fear and rage.

8

WHEN FAMILY MEMBERS APPEAR
Confronting a Furious Husband

Fairly early in my practice, in the 1960s, my wife started to receive in the mail newspaper obituaries of psychoanalysts and other therapists. Her name and address were typed, and the envelopes were all postmarked in Manhattan. She became extremely upset at receiving these notices because she felt my life was in jeopardy. The fact that her father had recently died compounded her distress.

She and I were both mystified as to who was sending these notices. At first I was not unduly alarmed because I thought the notices might have been sent by one of my adolescent patients. At that time about fifty percent of my practice consisted of children and adolescents, and the obituary notices looked to me like an adolescent prank. But I began to become upset at the relentlessness of the sender and at my wife's anxiety, which increased with each notice.

One day the mail brought my wife a package. She unwrapped it and discovered to her horror a fairly large doll with its head severed. She was frantic and I started to feel quite frantic myself. I faced one of the greatest dilemmas I had ever confronted as an analyst. On the one hand I wanted to ease my wife's suffering; on the other hand I felt helpless as to how to go about it.

I told myself it was preposterous to question each of my patients about this matter. Doing so would disrupt the therapeutic work: Who wants to be charged by his analyst with being a criminal? Furthermore, the culprit was not likely to admit his guilt.

I consulted the police and FBI, but they said no crime had been committed. I suggested death threats were implied (the severed head), but they disagreed. I felt more and more helpless and angrier and angrier. I thought I was not a very courageous husband and certainly not a competent therapist. I could not solve the problem; I kept wondering who the culprit was, but no satisfactory answer appeared, not even a clue.

Finally I got lucky: my would-be assassin unconsciously revealed himself. Many criminals, as Freud suggested, seek to be caught because their burden of guilt is unbearable.

One morning I noticed the latest obituary sent to my wife was cut out of a newspaper in southern Connecticut, though the envelope contained the usual Manhattan postmark. I played sleuth. Only one patient lived in Connecticut. She was in her late thirties, married to a wealthy real-estate broker. She was also currently engaged in an erotic transference to me (as I've said before, this is a part of almost every analysis). I was sure her husband was aware of this, because she had told me he wondered if she were having an affair with me.

I knew I had my man. My patient's husband thought I was taking his wife from him, and he wanted to take me away from her (and my wife) by informing me my life was at stake.

I felt many different emotions as I realized I had discovered the would-be assassin. I felt like a successful detective solving a crime, which gave me a feeling of elation, exultation, and pride. But I also felt confused. How was I going to stop this man from sending more obituary notices to my frightened wife? And could I stop him without placing myself, and his wife's treatment, in jeopardy? I was clearly most interested at this point in preserving my life.

I was very upset about the possibility that this man, whom I will call Robert Nelson, might have sinister plans for me. I had worked for years with men and women who had fantasies about destroying me, but Robert Nelson actually wanted me dead. With him it was more than a fantasy; he actually meant to destroy me.

As I reviewed my work with his wife, Donna, several issues became clear. First, I realized that, like most women who have jealous sexual partners, she unconsciously *wanted* her husband to compete with me, and in many ways she overtly and covertly stimulated him to go after me. Second, I have usually, if not always, found that when a man is obsessed with the notion that his wife or lover is having an affair, he usually has a deep interest in this "other man."

As I showed in my book *The Extra-Marital Affair*, whether an affair is real or a fantasy, there is usually unconscious collusion between husband and wife. Robert Nelson and Donna Nelson were both interested in the idea of my having an affair with Mrs. Nelson. Donna used me as a weapon to make her husband jealous. Robert got vicarious gratification from picturing his wife with me. Otherwise, why was he so obsessed with the imaginary liaison?

I realized Robert Nelson wanted contact with me—one way or another, peaceable or warlike—and I thought a face-to-face encounter might gratify him and might enable me to persuade him to stop his threats, perhaps even refer him to another analyst for treatment.

But my conflicts were many. Donna Nelson did not ask me to see her husband. She was enjoying a fantasy affair with me and was likely to resist my facing him. Clearly my wish to see her husband was not in the interest of her therapy. I also had to cope with the notion I was acting in my own interest.

For a number of days I wrestled with the possibility of meeting Robert Nelson, trying to rationalize it as therapeutic for both husband and wife. Finally I admitted I could not justify seeing Robert Nelson on a therapeutic basis. I told myself I would be doing it to protect myself and my wife and family. If my patient benefited, fine. But she might not. I had to know what I was doing.

One day while I was worrying about what to do, I heard Donna Nelson from the couch remark that whenever she functioned most easily, her husband felt worse. This happens frequently when one member of a family is in treatment and the other or others are not. The equilibrium of the Nelson marriage became upset when Mrs. Nelson began to feel less masochistic, and like herself more, as a result of our work. But she was also using me neurotically, making me a weapon she could employ psychologically to make her husband feel less competent.

She described a dream that clearly revealed her pleasure in using me as weapon against her husband: she fantasied me as a general who shot her husband. It became clear to both Mrs. Nelson and me that she enjoyed ganging up on her husband by using me to make him jealous.

As I helped her become aware of her unconscious wish to hurt her husband, she was able to accept my suggestion that perhaps it would be a good idea for him to see me for a consultation, with a view toward his going into treatment. She accepted almost everything I said as in her best interest. I then thought seriously of calling her husband.

But I had trouble accepting the idea of meeting him. I now strongly realized I would be seeing him for reasons that did not really relate to therapy. This troubled me because it conflicted with my professional standards and ethics. I became even more upset as I fantasied what might happen between Robert Nelson and myself. He was clearly feeling murderous at long-distance range. What would he feel when he was actually in my presence? And what would I do when I saw him? Would we engage in verbal and physical duels, as I had fantasied at times? (Sometimes I won, sometimes he won.)

As I analyzed my fantasies, I realized that however sinister and evil Robert Nelson might be, I was engaged in an oedipal battle with him. I was fighting with him over a woman I unconsciously wanted to win, an attractive woman, charming and intelligent.

I knew I was fighting Robert Nelson over two women— his wife and my wife. I was out to show him I was the better man. (I recalled the announcer in the World Championship Boxing Matches who would say, "May the better man win.") I further analyzed the battle as relating to my unconscious battle with my father as to who was "the better man" in the eyes of my mother and sister. This childhood battle now became quite real, perhaps more real than it had been at any other time in my adult life.

Finally, one evening, I dialed Robert Nelson at home. A deep masculine voice answered. I said, "This is Dr. Strean. I'd like to meet with you, Mr. Nelson."

There was a long silence. Then he said in a rather cool voice but with apparent interest, "When would you like to see me?"

"Is a week from Friday at ten A.M. convenient for you?"

After another long silence: "I think I can make it." He did not even ask why I wanted to see him. He was ready to meet me.

As the day grew nearer I became more and more anxious

about the interview. I realized Robert Nelson and I were both battling acute oedipal conflicts, approaching each other like gladiators. I was prepared not so much for an interview as for a fight. In many ways I felt like a boxer in training, flexing my psychological muscles, wondering where I would find my opponent's vulnerability and sock it to him. He had shown his desire to sever my head because I was working on his wife's head, so to speak, so I could legitimately view him as a bully. I realized further that, in seeing him, I was seeking revenge on any male who in reality or fantasy tried to bully me.

I prepared well for the battle. I gathered together all the obituary notices, now numbering in the dozens, as well as both parts of the doll. He had recently begun to send *in memoriam* cards to my wife, though she felt less threatened after I told her I was virtually positive I had my man and had set up a confrontation with him in my office.

On Thursday I told my colleague, with whom I share an office suite, about the next day's interview with Mr. Nelson and why I was seeing him. I asked my colleague, "Would you stand outside my door in case I need your help? I don't know what's going to happen." He arranged his schedule so he would be free at that hour. After he heard my office door shut behind Robert Nelson, he said, he would come and stand guard outside my closed door, ready to come to my rescue if he heard me shout for help.

I wanted Robert Nelson to know there was another analyst at work in the office suite. If he had a gun, he might not use it if he knew someone was near at hand and could identify him. But nothing in my analytic studies, my pursuit of psychoanalytic literature, my many years of personal analysis, prepared me for this encounter. I was very frightened, and I admitted my fear to myself and my colleague.

About fifteen minutes before Mr. Nelson was due, he phoned. "I'm not sure if I have your correct address. Are you on Ninety-sixth Street?"

I gave him my address, though I was sure the call was just an attempt to throw me off balance. On many occasions he had driven his wife to her sessions and waited for her downstairs, parked outside the front door.

Before his arrival, I placed the obituary notices and other items in full view on my desk. As he walked into the room, he could hardly fail to see them.

When I first saw Robert Nelson in the waiting room, my knees buckled, my heart started to beat faster, and I began gasping for breath. He was six feet five inches tall—six inches taller than I—and he weighed at least 250 pounds. If I'd had fantasies of beating him up, they were swiftly punctured at the sight of him. He had a rugged face and broad shoulders, wore an expensive gray suit, and possessed what I have described as a "paranoid stare"—in other words, he looked ready for combat, angry at the world.

My buckling knees, fast-beating heart, and heavy breathing were clearly the responses of a man who knows he is about to be knocked out—a middleweight up against a heavyweight.

I said, with what breath I could muster, "Please come into my office," and led him down the hall.

He entered, took one look at the obituary notices and other materials I had laid out on the desk, and bellowed, "Are you accusing me of something?"

I immediately knew I had my man. Only he would have recognized those items and their menacing content. He was ready to be accused as soon as he walked into my office. Only a frightened, guilty person would accuse me of wanting to accuse him of "something."

He started to walk out of the office. Though my knees were still shaking and my heart fluttering, I said, louder and more firmly than I have ever spoken as an analyst before or since: "Sit down!"

To my surprise, he meekly turned around and sat in the patient's chair, thoroughly filling it. He appeared at that moment less like a six-foot-five-inch 250-pound gladiator and more like a little boy submitting to his intimidating father. As he sat down and I felt how basically vulnerable and emotionally fragile he was, my anger, competitiveness, and wish to defeat him seemed to vanish. But I knew I had to put some limits on this "little boy" at once.

I said, "These obituary notices"—pointing to the stack— "and the other mailings"—referring primarily to the beheaded doll—"have to stop."

He protested, "Don't accuse me of anything. I didn't do that."

In his protestation Robert Nelson reminded me of a child caught in the middle of a delinquent act. He protested, but the protest did not ring true.

I ignored his denial. "You'll go to jail or a mental hospital if you don't stop this harassment."

He again protested, but more feebly, "I didn't do it."

The sudden pathos in his rugged face convinced me he was feeling some anguish and despair. Sometimes one is tempted to remain in battle after one's enemy is vanquished, but my therapist's convictions helped me resist this temptation.

I said, "Mr. Nelson, you appear to be a troubled man. I think you're very upset about your wife's treatment with me. I believe you're worried I'm going to take her away from you rather than help her enjoy her life with you."

I was startled to see tears in the eyes of this hulk of a man. He took out his handkerchief, blew his nose, then asked in a subdued voice, "Do you know somebody who can help me?"

At that moment I sensed he wished to be mothered more than anything else in the world. I asked, "Would you prefer a man or a woman therapist?"

"You decide," he said.

I wrote down the name and address of a woman psychoanalyst; he accepted it gratefully.

Then he stood up, said, "Thank you, Dr. Strean." He put out his large right hand and shook my no longer trembling one.

As the outer door closed behind him, I went into my colleague's office, to which he had fled when he heard Mr. Nelson open my door.

"How are you?" I asked. I had the feeling he might be more upset than I was, listening to the dramatic encounter through the closed door.

He looked pale but relieved the battle was ended.

Robert Nelson started to see the analyst I had suggested. His wife became more aware of her contributions to their marital difficulties. I realized that though consciously she professed love for me, she also wished to exploit me in her war with her husband. She used me to express her hatred for him and used him to express her hatred toward me. She wanted us to beat each other up so she could feel she had triumphed over both of us.

I learned from this case that when a family member opposes the therapist, the patient plays a role in the opposition. Until my work with Donna Nelson, I had a tendency to regard people like her as victims when, in reality, the patient is an active participant in all marital difficulties and in every therapeutic impasse.

Ever since then, when a patient tells me a member of his family is against the therapy, I know the patient is using the relative's antagonism to covertly express his own. It is my job, when a patient informs me someone opposes his therapy, to help the patient recognize his own resistance to treatment.

If I were working with a Donna Nelson today, I would try to avoid the altercation with her husband. I would show Donna Nelson, as she talked of her husband's anger at me, that in many ways this represented her anger at me and she enjoyed externalizing her hostility toward men rather than facing it.

I also realized a part of me was all too ready to join with her in fighting her husband. Experience and greater self-awareness have tempered my understanding sufficiently so that today, when a patient claims a relative opposes his therapy, I help the patient become aware of his own investment in his fight against self-awareness. If I had been more experienced, I would have helped Mrs. Nelson persuade her husband to enter treatment so there would have been no need for me to meet him and risk possible fisticuffs—a risk that, I realize in hindsight, attracted me unconsciously because I was all too ready to enjoy a fight.

Relatives of patients frequently get in touch with the analyst, but this dimension of the analyst's work is seldom discussed in the psychoanalytic literature.

A number of issues remain similarly unclear to this day, perhaps because the founder of psychoanalysis himself was unsure about how to handle them. On the one hand, Freud said, "Above all, our interests will be directed toward the family circumstances of our patients," but on the other hand, he admitted that family members were troublesome to the analyst. In dealing with family members, he said, the analyst feels like a surgeon when strangers look over his shoulder during an operation.

Yet at times Freud worked directly with a family member to help a patient. In 1909 he used the father of "Little Hans," who had a phobia about horses, as "go-between" therapist after the father went to Freud's office for consultation on a weekly basis. At other times, however, Freud referred to family members as "enemies" of the patient's treatment, warning analysts to remain aloof from them.

Freud's ambivalence toward family members is still in evidence within the psychoanalytic profession. Some psychoanalysts will never see or speak to the spouse, parent, or child of a patient. Others will treat married couples jointly, and still others will treat an entire family, parents and children together.

Most analysts agree that when one member of a family is in treatment and starts to change—to become less depressed, for example—other members will be affected. When I first started working with children, most of the time I saw the child alone. After the mother gave me details on the child's background, she was banished to the waiting room. But I learned, as did my colleagues, that if a child started to show therapeutic gains, the mother often unconsciously tried to sabotage those gains. If a passive, effeminate boy became more assertive and aggressive, this threatened the mother, who unconsciously had given her son "love premiums" for being passive and effeminate—otherwise he would not have been that way in the first place. Or if a daughter who had been very clinging started to become, through therapy, more autonomous, this new independence might threaten the mother who unconsciously had rewarded her daughter for being dependent to an extreme degree. In the early 1950s, I read articles and heard child guidance experts say, "Mothers are patients, too." It became clear to those of us who worked with children that unless mothers were involved in treatment for themselves, a child's therapeutic gains could never be sustained. I also recall an article in the mid-fifties called "Mother and Child Get Better: Father Gets Worse." Father, it seemed, needed help, too.

I led one of the first fathers' groups in the child guidance clinic of the Jewish Board of Guardians in the 1950s. Staff members referred to my group as "the garbage of the agency"—in those days, contempt for fathers was strong. But slowly and surely people began to recognize the importance of fathers, and the evolution of family therapy in the early 1960s was predictable. Today more and more psychoanalytically oriented therapists recognize the importance of both mother and father. But many others, like Freud, still regard a patient's parent or spouse as an enemy looking over their shoulder.

When I hear from a family member, I know something is happening to the patient. If a husband on the couch is making progress, his wife will be affected and will react. If a man who has always been passive and inhibited starts to assert himself sexually, this new behavior may upset his wife, particularly if she is not in treatment. The same can be said for the husband whose inhibited, frightened wife suddenly feels freer sexually.

Because I became so convinced that a shift in attitude and behavior on the part of a child could shake up the equilibrium of parents, it was easy for me to see how the same phenomenon might occur in a marriage or in any other family relationship. I have noted many times that when a patient changes during therapy, even his friends react, sometimes with anger. People become friends because a certain bond exists between them, based on their idiosyncracies and conflicts—birds of a psychic feather flock together. Therefore if a person changes in attitude or behavior, his friends inevitably feel anxious. Some patients as they gain more self-esteem even give up a friend who has treated them hostilely.

Few analysts or therapists of any orientation would disagree with the assertion that change in one member of a family induces concern and sometimes distress in another, but they disagree about what they should do when that family member phones them or wants to see them. Those analysts who oppose any contact with a family member can legitimately say the patient's treatment will be affected if a spouse, parent, child, or other relative consults the analyst. Many patients feel extremely upset about sharing their analyst with a "rival" for even one session. For instance, if a sibling appears on the scene, treatment can halt or go downhill. Even patients who know a casual friend is in treatment with their analyst react strongly. Thus bringing in a family member can be quite disruptive for some patients. Also, many patients are somewhat suspicious and distrustful, and the knowledge that the analyst is seeing a family member can intensify their suspicion and distrust. An analyst also may lose some of his objectivity after seeing a relative. These are only a few of the reasons why an analyst might object to talking with a family member.

On the positive side, however, there are good reasons to support the family-member consultation. When mothers and fathers see their child's therapist, for example, they are often relieved to learn that they need not take all the blame, that the child himself plays a part in the family difficulties. Husbands and wives who go to the same therapist can also learn about shared blame and mutual responsibility for family problems. A therapist can get a better understanding of certain problems if he sees both husband and wife or parents and child. In the few times I treated husband and wife in separate therapy, I have been shocked at how frequently each distorts arguments and fails to see the other objectively.

I believe that there are valid arguments on both sides of this issue. But I also believe that the analyst's decision to see or not to see a relative has more to do with the therapist's own defenses, fantasies, and beliefs than with those of the patient. More often than not, the analyst uses theory to protect and reinforce what makes him comfortable. I have heard therapists and marriage counselors argue with analysts about this issue, and it seems clear to me that their theoretical differences often mask their own anxieties and protect their own vulnerabilities.

Like most other analysts, I have found myself going back and forth on this issue. I suspect that my shifts, like those of other analysts, had a good deal to do with what was going on inside me. Also at times I realized I wanted to rescue one family member from another, and this urge motivated me to see a relative of a patient.

At this point in my professional development I believe the decision about seeing family members has to be made on an individual basis. At certain times treatment of a family member will be helpful; at other times it will be detrimental. If a husband and wife or a parent and child are extremely close, separating them, asking them to see different therapists, could be too traumatic; they may need the same analyst. Or, when an individual has achieved good results with an analyst, the spouse may want the same analyst. If the two individuals are sufficiently aware of their feelings so they do not have to fight it out like angry siblings, I do not see any harm in going to the same analyst. At the same time, if a child or a spouse wants to keep me all to himself or herself, I respect this. With certain patients who feel their parents have sided with a brother or sister, it is not advisable for the analyst to take on a family member.

Ultimately, however, the decision is based on the analyst's inner comfort or discomfort. He must subject his own inclinations or disinclinations to self-analysis before making the decision. If I am working with an attractive woman who is married and whose husband wants to enter treatment with me, I must deal with my wish to be number one man and with my rivalry with her husband. If I am treating a husband and the wife wants to start treatment with me, I have to deal with my resistance to the wife, since I unconsciously see her as my mother, trying to interfere during a tête-à-tête between me and my father. Many times in working with children I have noted my competition with parents and my wish to be the child's adoptive or foster parent. This has contributed to my reluctance at times to see parents of a child.

But for the most part I have enjoyed my role as big brother and family peacemaker when called on to use it in psychotherapy. This stems from my success in arbitrating arguments between my parents. I recall a day when I was six and my parents were planning one of their many moves to another house. My mother wanted to sell the kitchen linoleum for six dollars to the new tenant. My father insisted the amount was excessive—it should be five dollars (this was 1937, during the depression). Listening to my parents feuding and fussing, I finally said, "Why not make it five dollars and fifty cents?" They agreed on this as an acceptable compromise. This was typical of many other childhood feuds in which I emerged as peacemaker. Later in life I often served as a peacemaker in professional societies and psychoanalytic institutes.

The role of arbiter has remained with me all my life in many varied situations. Therefore I feel reasonably comfortable when I find myself in the middle of a family fracas. I know the role of peacemaker usually evolves out of conflict: I went back and forth in my loyalties toward my mother and father when they argued—sometimes feeling uncomfortable about identifying with father against mother, sometimes with mother against father.

To defend against my own hostile and competitive fantasies, the peacemaker role has often been a comfortable compromise. But, as with everything else, it too has to be subjected to constant analysis. As with all issues in psychoanalysis, the analyst's emotional state is one of the most potent variables in deciding which way to move with family members.

9

THE CASE OF THE PERPLEXED POET
Treating a Gay Patient

Into my office one day about ten years ago walked a tall bearded man in his late twenties. He was dressed in immaculate white slacks, a brown shirt, and an obviously expensive beige sweater. He wore tennis shoes and looked very much the laid-back artist. He had called in advance for a consultation. His name was Stephen Morgan.

He now announced, "I'm giving some thought to going into psychoanalysis, though I have a lot of doubts." Those doubts, he explained, arose from his earlier experience with another analyst. He said, "I felt this analyst wanted me to submit to him too quickly. He asked me to come to his office four times a week and to start at once."

I kept silent, waited for him to go on.

He explained, "The last thing in the world I want is to have someone tell me how to live. My father did this all my life. I rebel whenever anyone orders me to do something. I want to make up my own mind."

He peered into my eyes as though wishing to make an important point. "I am a poet, and most of my poetry is full of thoughts of revenge and hatred toward those who try to order other people around. That's what is wrong with the world."

His next association was about his father: "My father is a wealthy doctor with middle-class values. He thinks of achievement in terms of making money or being important in the world of sports, like a Joe DiMaggio or a Mickey Mantle—all things I abhor. I chose poetry as a career to defy my father, because nobody makes much money writing poems. I refuse to be money hungry like him."

Then he announced, much to my surprise, for he had talked of his father as if he were still living, "My father died three months ago." He added quickly, "I'm not sure this has anything to do with my sudden depression, though the other analyst said it did. But I now have trouble eating, sleeping, and even writing poetry. My father left me quite a lot of money, so I don't have to worry about making a living."

He was silent for a few moments, then said, "I have to take care of my mother who's in a deep depression, though I don't know why. She loathed my father and his values. She's a very controlling woman. She reigned over our house like a queen. Looks on me as her baby prince."

He added grimly, "I've hated her at times because, like my father, she'd never let me stand on my own two feet. I had to obey and cater to both my parents."

"Do you have any brothers or sisters?" I asked.

"I have a sister, Grace, three years younger. My feelings about her are mixed. As kids we played a lot. I always felt my parents loved her more. She didn't have to work as hard as I did to get some expression of their love." He sighed, "Such as it was."

Then, not looking into my eyes but at the floor: "There's something that embarasses me to tell you. But I have to be fair so you'll know all about me. I have had sex only twice in my life."

And then, still not raising his eyes: "Both times with a man."

I said not a word. He looked into my eyes, then asked suspiciously, "What do you think of that?"

This was the same question every homosexual in treatment with me had asked. It held a strong implication: You think homosexuality is awful, and you want me to be a heterosexual, don't you?

By the time I met Stephen I had learned that every homosexual patient suspects the analyst will try to force him into heterosexuality, and he hates the analyst for "forcing" him, as Stephen's father had "forced" him all his life, telling him what to do. Yet frequently the homosexual patient also unconsciously hopes the analyst will lead him to a heterosexual life so he will feel more like a man.

Few homosexuals, however, come to analysis with the conscious wish to give up their homosexuality. Like Stephen, a crisis occurs in their lives—the loss of a parent or a lover, or perhaps a work conflict that causes them to feel depressed. Homosexuality is rarely what therapists call "the presenting problem."

The vast majority of homosexual patients want analysis to lessen stress, depression, or unhappiness; on the conscious level, at least, they wish to keep their sexual way of life.

When Stephen said, "What do you think of that?" I realized he was trying to see where I stood. I said, "You're worried about what I will think of you because of your sexual life. Isn't that it?"

He then said exactly what I thought he would say: "I'm worried you won't approve of my sex life. I'm afraid you'll force me to have sex with women as soon as possible."

I suggested, "Perhaps you're experiencing me as a pressuring father who tells you how to live."

"You're not?" he asked, then laughed with relief.

He obviously welcomed my words. "There's a big difference between you and the analyst I just left: you don't judge me." He was silent again, then announced, "I'd like to go into analysis with you."

My ability to help a homosexual man feel accepted, not judged, was long in coming. At the start of practice, I was not successful in keeping homosexual men in treatment for long. At first I rationalized my failures by telling myself these men were "poorly motivated," difficult to treat, too resistant to being helped. But after a while I realized these were rationalizations. I had to look deeper into myself.

As I have already suggested, no analyst can help a patient resolve difficulties the analyst has not resolved in himself. Therefore, for me to help a Stephen, I had to look at the homosexual in myself and accept what Freud said many decades ago: there is both a man and a woman in all of us.

As I thought over parts of my life while listening to Stephen in this first consultation, I realized once again that the similarities between analyst and patient are far greater than the differences. It is extremely important for every analyst to be able to recognize these similarities. In my early years as a therapist I thought of myself as "different" from homosexuals, and they sensed this. They experienced my defensiveness and smugness and left treatment prematurely, just as Stephen left the analyst he had seen earlier.

At the time he consulted me, society, psychoanalysts, and civil libertarians were rethinking the issue of homosexuality. Civil libertarians were correctly pointing out that homosexual men and women were being discriminated against and used as scapegoats. Many sectors of society were trying to accept the differences, including sexual differences, between people. Analysts, though often accused of living in an ivory tower, were rethinking their positions on homosexuality. Some joined the psychiatrists in agreeing to strike the label "homosexuality" from psychiatric manuals.

At the time I saw Stephen, I was writing an article entitled "Homosexuality: A Life Style, a Civil Rights Issue, or a Psychosocial Problem?" In it I urged all mental health professionals to become more understanding of the many patients whose life styles differ markedly from their own: gay people, feminists, single parents, unmarried couples who lived together, swingers, switchers.

I also pointed out that mental health professionals had to differentiate civil rights issues from psychological problems. I believed mental health professionals—in their attempt to protect the right to self-determination of homosexual patients and accept their uniqueness, dignity, and worth—often overlooked the terrors and conflicts in the lives of homosexual patients.

While many mental health professionals would disagree, I maintain that exclusive homosexuality is rarely found among those who have had consistently gratifying love experiences with their parents. Homosexual patients often attest to the fact that a total rejection of the opposite sex usually comes out of a background of severe childhood emotional deprivation. Often when an analyst closely examines a homosexual couple, he sees deep vulnerability, uncertainty, and desire for revenge in both partners.

As I have examined the nature of the wish for revenge, I have frequently observed it contains the feelings Stephen mentioned. He was furious at both parents for not accepting him as he was but imposing on him their rules and way of life. Virtually every homosexual patient I have treated has told me he considers his sexual life a way of telling his parents to go to hell.

While I was treating a homosexual patient in the 1960s, Mayor John Lindsay of New York worked actively to provide homosexuals and lesbians with more civil rights in jobs and housing. I thought my patient would be pleased with this, but instead, he told me something I will never forget. He said, "If they're going to treat me as an equal, and Lindsay certainly seems to want to do that, who will I rebel against and how will I express my wish for revenge?"

This patient taught me about the deep rage in almost anyone who chooses homosexuality. I became aware of the profound psychic agony and conflict that forced this man to be constantly at war with his parents and with society. I learned that the pain of the homosexual is usually quite acute. This pain is associated with a feeling that may emerge partially out of fantasy but is usually based on a modicum of fact—the fact that one parent or both in some way demolished him emotionally in childhood. It may have been a subtle demolition rather than an overt one, but it is intense and lasting.

The desire for revenge stems from fury at being overcontrolled and overpowered and then being forced to contain the fury, as well as from the bondage that the overcontrol and overpowering induces. Invariably I have noted the homosexual man is so full of violent fantasies and so frightened of these fantasies that he will unconsciously weaken himself rather than risk punishment for expressing his intense hatred. Many homosexual men choose to identify with women and emotionally castrate themselves in order to evade the deeper psychological pain that would arise from acting out this hatred.

Often psychoanalysts are asked, "Why do you have such dogmatic views on homosexuality? Don't you realize you work from a skewed sample—those in treatment?"

When I am asked this question, I point out that those who go into treatment are indeed a skewed sample: they are more mature than those who do not have the courage to confront themselves and face their distorted fantasies and irrationalities so they can live more happily. Many lay people and even some professionals assume a person who is in distress and who seeks therapy is less mature than the person who stubbornly ignores his tormenting conflicts. I have felt for a long time that feeling stress about a problem may be viewed as healthier than apparent lack of distress about that same problem. Some of the homosexual men and women who repudiate their need for therapy may feel so vulnerable, so frightened of facing their inner conflicts, that they must deny them, repress their fearful feelings.

These were some of my thoughts as I began work with Stephen Morgan. He took to treatment like the proverbial duck to water, enjoyed being listened to empathically. As he described his childhood, he contrasted me with his parents. He said, "They were completely absorbed in themselves. They never heard a word I said, even when I read them my poetry. You really listen."

I could identify strongly with Stephen because I, too, experienced my parents as extremely narcissistic. I felt that they found it difficult to understand me. I grew stronger emotionally when my analyst patiently listened to me, and I learned to appreciate the value of what Dr. Reuben Fine calls "dynamic inactivity"—an exchange wherein the analyst carefully and empathically listens and the patient does most of the talking.

Stephen liked talking so much that after two months of three times a week on the chair, he suggested he lie down on the couch. He explained, "I might relax more and talk more if I'm stretched out on my back."

Usually it takes longer for a working relationship to be established so that the patient trusts me without seeing me, feels secure enough to lie down and regress, let his thoughts fly wherever they wish, usually back to childhood memories.

But Stephen was an exception. He felt so accepted and appreciated by me that he wanted to lie on the couch, though I had been careful not to push him to do so.

Stephen continued his "honeymoon" with me after he started lying down during his sessions. But I have often said, and other analysts agree, that a honeymoon cannot last forever. As Stephen continued in his analysis, he stopped wanting to be "listened to," he started to hate talking, and the couch became a chore. Instead of feeling comfortable in reporting dreams, he felt it an onerous burden. Instead of seeing me as a kind, beneficent father figure, he called me a tyrant and said I reminded him of Hitler.

"You hardly say anything. You make me do all the work," he charged. "You are an icy, unfriendly man. You are only interested in turning me into a heterosexual like yourself."

He spent whole sessions lambasting me, criticizing me, and questioning the validity of psychoanalysis. At times he sounded like an attorney demanding that I prove the case for psychoanalysis. When I pointed out his desire to debate with me rather than reveal himself, he countered, "You're always trying to cover your ass."

That last charge held many meanings for a homosexual, but it was too early to discuss those meanings with him. I have learned when a patient is full of rage this is rarely the time for interpretations or deeper probing. The rage must be discharged first. When the patient sees the analyst accept his anger instead of being repulsed by it, interpretation may follow. Some analysts use interpretations to engage in combat with their patients, and I confess that I sometimes did that years ago, particularly with homosexual men.

In the past I had failed to understand that all homosexual men hold deep resentment toward their fathers and that they are bound to hurl this resentment at the analyst. If the analyst cannot tolerate a patient's wish to demean or castrate him, the analyst may resort to striking back with an interpretation. Analysts, like all human beings, try to protect themselves from these blows and may do so by using psychoanalytic jargon as psychic bullets, especially when a homosexual man tries to place the analyst in the sort of weak, vulnerable position he feels he is in. Unless the analyst can empathically relate to the patient's feelings, treatment will not be successful.

By the time I worked with Stephen in the middle 1970s, I felt more secure about myself, much less vulnerable as a man and as an analyst. Thus I was not particularly threatened by his animosity but could empathize with it. I told myself that Stephen felt weak and castrated and therefore wanted to put me in that position, too. I would help him with his anger at me.

Stephen slowly realized I did not want to argue or fight with him as his father had done. When I told him I was not there to fight him, he asked, as he had in the first interview, "You mean you aren't?"

He found it difficult to believe I was trying to help him understand himself better, that I was not trying to manipulate him—as both parents had done. He recalled memories in which both his mother and father, as well as teachers and other parental figures, tried to mold him into the kind of person they wished him to be, instead of allowing him to develop freely into his own person. I believe he thought I wanted to turn him into a duplicate Herb Strean.

This conflict exists in all analytic relationships and all parent-child relationships. Every parent holds hopes, wishes, and expectations for a child, and every child has mixed feelings about these parental aspirations. A child wants to please his parents but also feels like rebelling against parental edicts. To a patient, the analyst seems like a parent who wants to impose new values on him. The patient faces a conflict between his wish to please and his wish to rebel.

This was the plight of Stephen. He consciously rebelled against being too strongly influenced by me, but he also had a strong wish to be my "little boy," to become a replica of me. He found this wish to be my son stimulating but also frightening. He wanted me to take care of him, but he was also in a rage because he felt small and vulnerable.

When I did not respond to his hostility and when he decided I was not trying to turn him into a Strean clone, he allowed himself to get in touch with his wish to be a small boy with me. He became conscious of fantasies of sitting on my lap, being adopted by me. When I heard him describe these fantasies, I appreciated how deeply and keenly he felt them. I, too, had yearnings to be loved by a strong father, could empathize with Stephen's wish.

But I also knew from my training and personal analysis that to gratify his wishes would keep him a little boy, prevent him from maturing. Instead, I had to act in a way it had taken me a long time to learn: when a patient tearfully and with agitation wishes me to be a supportive parental figure, I listen empathically and help him understand his resistance to growing up—a most difficult task for the patient and a most difficult task for many analysts.

As he tried to lure me into becoming mother and father to him, Stephen noted I did not say much. He raged, "You're just a cold Freudian. You're not interested in being kind or understanding. I feel I am in court being charged with all kinds of crimes. Last night I dreamed I was a defendant and you were the prosecutor." Then he complained, "My analysis is making me feel worse instead of helping me. All you want is to earn money and to prove your stupid theories."

He started to complain of physical symptoms, suffered insomnia—a new ailment for him—lost his appetite, and shed pounds. He announced he felt more depressed than when he entered treatment shortly after his father's death. He had been unable for weeks to write a line of poetry.

This was a difficult time for me. I saw a man suffering, unable to eat or sleep, his work deteriorating. I was tempted many times to offer supportive and reassuring remarks that would temporarily diminish his depression and underlying rage. But I also knew Stephen was trying to manipulate me into being an omnipotent father so as to keep himself a little boy. To gratify this wish would have been a mistake. Thus the wrestling match within me between what Freud called "the surgeon" versus the humane, parental figure was settled: I wanted to help Stephen mature, even as I wanted to alleviate his pain.

During this period in Stephen's analysis I was reminded of the many times I had frustrated my own children when I helped them grow by dealing with their anger at me. I also recalled the many times I sought reassurance when I was analyzed and later realized had it been given, I would have remained a young boy emotionally, unable to accept the natural frustrations of existence.

I explained to Stephen that he hoped his suffering would persuade me to take care of him. He broke out into intense rage, told me, "You deserve to die. You are one of the cruelest human beings I have ever met."

He threatened to leave treatment, even sought consultation with a woman therapist. But when she told him that, though I had a fine reputation, she could help him even more, he became suspicious of her. He returned to me, explained that as much as he hated me, "You're not a charlatan all the time. And you would never criticize a fellow analyst the way this woman criticized you. She sounded like my mother berating my father."

His meeting with the woman therapist was both a turning point in his analysis and a chance to clarify how he felt about treatment by me. On the one hand, he wanted to be my young son and hated me for not gratifying this wish. On the other hand, when he started to feel like my young son, he hated me because he felt so inferior. When he hated me as a son, either the son who was frustrated or the son who felt belittled, he wanted to attack and destroy me. Then he felt very guilty for his rage and frightened at the possible loss of his father figure.

These themes continued to be part of our analytic work for some time. As Stephen felt more and more understood by me and gained more understanding of himself, he became emotionally stronger. His poetry achieved national recognition, he was even acclaimed internationally, and he found himself a popular lecturer. He told me some friends who knew him before analysis commented on how different he appeared—more confident, more spontaneous, more caring. But he was quick to say his growth was independent of me, assured me, "You have had a limited, if any, impact on my change."

As he began to feel new strength, he became contemptuous of me. He belittled me as a man and analyst, announced he was vastly superior to me in every area of living and working. Knowing I was also a professor, he informed me he had started to teach, and said he was more competent than I. He also said scornfully that if he were married to my wife, she would undoubtedly be much more responsive sexually to him than to me.

For the first time in his life Stephen flirted with and dated women, though he did not have sex with them. He rationalized this fear of sex by saying, "It would tie me down." His dreams and fantasies revealed he was making the women into mothers and feeling like a little boy about to be emotionally devoured.

I enjoyed Stephen's wish to compete with me. It reminded me of times I welcomed my sons beating me in Ping-Pong or basketball. Having sufficiently come to grips with my oedipal conflict, I did not particularly feel threatened by Stephen's wish to take away my wife or to kill me. The threats were old hat; I had been through this many times with young boys and adult males I had treated, as well as in my own analysis.

As Stephen's oedipal conflicts emerged in the analysis and as his life story unfolded, I appreciated as never before Freud's explanation of the cause of male homosexuality. As Stephen competed with me, he recalled memories of lying in bed with his mother and how excited he felt to be so near her body. He also remembered sex play with his sister and two girls in the neighborhood.

He then brought up memories of times when he had felt like destroying his father and marrying his mother, recalled how terrified and guilty he felt. To reduce his guilt over murderous and incestuous wishes, at the age of eleven he fantasied himself as a girl married to her father or a father figure.

These fantasies showed precisely what Freud called the cause of male homosexuality: the boy feels so frightened and guilty about his incestuous and murderous thoughts that in fantasy he castrates himself (the punishment he fears because of his incestuous wishes about his mother) and submits to his father.

In his analysis Stephen now began to show the part of himself that wanted to become my wife or daughter, though this was difficult for him to put into words. In one session he wept, saying he felt bad about having expressed the wish I would die, because he loved me so much. He described a dream in which I lay beside him in a bed. As he moved toward me sexually, my wife walked into the room and pushed him away from me. He could not as yet accept how much he competed with my wife for my love, just as he competed with his mother for his father's love, but it was clear he desperately wanted my love.

One of the most difficult things for a male homosexual to do is to permit himself to feel sexual toward a male analyst. Stephen often said condescendingly, "You are not my type."

One day after he made this remark I asked, "What is your type?"

He replied, "A married man who is not effeminate and whom I can look to as a father for guidance and understanding."

I thought this described me fairly well; he was telling me I was not his type to ward off what he was eventually able to say: "If I become sexual with you, I'll want to have sex with you all day long, day in and day out."

When I explored with Stephen this intense wish to merge with me, he once again pushed me away, tried to devalue me. Frequently, throughout the analysis he tried to antagonize me in order to ward off loving feelings. Since I did not rebuke or criticize him, he could eventually acknowledge his wish to be my sexual partner as well as my little child.

When Stephen realized I neither gratified his wish to be child or lover, nor fought with him when he competed with me, he started to look at his life in greater emotional depth. He became aware he had spent so many hours alone because he was both frightened of intimacy and anxious about competition. It was less competitive for him to be a poet alone in his room than a doctor besieged by patients, like his father. Stephen could understand *why* he had to compete so strongly with his father and how this competition drove him to regress into what he believed to be the safer state of a loner. He also became aware that because he did not compete, he felt inferior and weak, then hated himself.

These insights helped him move more and more toward women. He was finally able to accept emotionally and sexually fulfilling moments with a woman. His professional life brought a good income as poet and lecturer and he became even more famous. He never worried about money because his father had left him a large inheritance, but the success of his poetry gave him a sense of identity.

We approached the last stage of his therapy. As he became even better known, he worried about how jealous I felt, how weak and impotent next to him. While I reassured myself Stephen's fears represented his wishes to surpass his father, I had to consider seriously what envy I did possess.

I dealt here with another issue rarely faced in psychoanalysis—the analyst's envy of and competition with the patient. Stephen's fame certainly was something I aspired to, and clearly he had achieved a celebrity status far surpassing mine. A few times, both in and out of sessions, I realized I would like to have his income, achieve his prominence. I moved toward resolving this tension within myself when, one day, during a session he asked, "How come I am so much more successful and famous than you?"

I maintained silence, but I was thinking, *Because you have a better analyst than I did.* I kept my competitive fantasies toward Stephen, and toward my analyst, to myself, though I realized Stephen's competition with me and wish to surpass me was a mirror of probably the most salient issue in my own personal analysis and in life with my father and father figures.

It has never been easy for me, as it obviously was not for Stephen, to temper my competitiveness toward father figures. I will say, though, that after many years of personal analysis and analytic work, I am now far more able to identify with a patient's successes, much as I identify with my sons' achievements. You reach a point in your development at which your children's, your students' and your patients' achievements become to some extent your own and the jealous child within you becomes a little tamer and much quieter.

I have found this to be true of myself as I reach the stage Erik Erikson refers to as "generativity." This occurs when the adult, instead of continuing to wish to be a perpetual child to whom all things are given, now gives to and loves others. We also call this "maturity."

10

THE PATIENT'S RESPONSE TO THE ANALYST'S UNCONSCIOUS
The Man Who Seemed to Read My Mind

One of the major tasks of the analyst is to listen carefully to the patient's thoughts, feelings, fantasies, and dreams. As the analyst hears the patient's associations, he in turn associates to them. A good analyst is always probing his own unconscious in an attempt to understand the deeper, or unconscious, meaning of the patient's utterances, then help the patient understand.

Perhaps the best way to determine what lies in the patient's unconscious is through the study of dreams, which reveal the secrets of the mind. The overt or "manifest" content of a dream is but a screen for the "latent," or unconscious, content. The analyst should always ask himself, "What does

---

the patient *really* (un-really) mean by that?" Even the public is aware of this, as shown in the joke about the two analysts who meet in the elevator. As one asks the other, "How are you this morning?" the other thinks, "I wonder what he means by that?"

If a patient says to the analyst, "I love you," the analyst does not think, Well, why not? I'm a lovable fellow trying to help him. Instead, he listens to the tone the patient uses when professing love. He assesses the thoughts that preceded the statement of love. He watches the patient's bodily movements as he speaks of love. The analyst also studies his own reaction when the patient makes the declaration of love.

Much has been written about how the analyst tries his best to be sensitive to the patient's unconscious wishes, hopes, fantasies, defenses, and blind spots, but little has been said about the patient's ability to "tune in" to the analyst's hopes, wishes, and anxieties. Just as children become sensitive to their parents' unconscious messages, I believe a patient may become attuned to the analyst's unconscious messages.

When a child hears a mother say repeatedly, "Be careful when you walk down the stairs that you don't fall and break your neck," he begins to recognize the parent's unconscious wish that the child fall downstairs and break his neck.

So, too, in analysis. When the patient hears, over and over from the analyst, sometimes reproachfully, "You fail to recognize your sexual fantasies toward me," the patient may believe the analyst feels unloved and is looking for some acknowledgment of him as a sexual being. If the patient wants the analyst's love, he may then start to consider the analyst as a sexual person, try to make him feel sexual, just as a child tries to fulfill a parent's unconscious wish so as to make the parent happy.

An eminent analyst, the late Dr. Ralph Greenson, gave a striking example of one patient's sensitivity to him. The patient said he knew Dr. Greenson was a liberal Democrat.

Dr. Greenson asked how the patient knew this. The patient replied, "Whenever I praise a Republican, you tell me I'm looking for an idealized father. Whenever I criticize Franklin D. Roosevelt, you tell me he reminds me of someone I hated in my past."

Though Greenson, master psychoanalytic technician, had been completely unaware of his unconscious revelations to the patient, it became evident to him that his tone, his questions, and his silences had helped the patient figure out his political bias.

All patients are eager to know, and make every effort to know, what the analyst likes and dislikes. This has been an important issue for me because long before I knew what psychoanalysis was all about, I tried to surmise what my parents wanted or did not want. To cope with the tensions in my own childhood family, I sensitized myself to my parents' unconscious messages. I learned, for example, that behind everything my father said to me was the message: "Be the best, be the strongest, be the most potent, be the most intellectual—but never be better than I am." My mother's unconscious message to me was this: "I'll love you if you don't become too strong, too competent, too athletic. Try to be like your sister; then I'll love you." Obviously these messages were contradictory and aroused deep conflict in me. My major coping device was to sensitize myself to my parents' unconscious wishes, try to give each what he or she wanted.

This strong relatedness to another person's unconscious showed itself many times in my personal analysis. As silent as my analyst was, I always knew I could draw some kind of response when I talked about lessening my hatred and increasing my loving feelings. I also knew if I accepted reality as it was, rather than as I wished it to be—recognizing that a colleague was hostile toward me and that I could not change that, for example—my analyst would in one way or another show a positive response.

Sensitivity to the other person's feelings had always helped me as a student. I could usually predict what a teacher wanted or what a professor would ask on an examination. In my own psychoanalytic training, I always knew what senior analysts wanted to hear and usually gave it to them quite eloquently.

Because of my interest in unconscious communication and my efforts to understand the unconscious of my own parents, teachers, and analyst, I became interested in how much my patients picked up about me. Some patients, I had noticed, confidently told me things about my life, my values, my biases, and proved remarkably correct.

While I was a student analyst in the late 1950s, I treated a man three times a week who, more than any patient I have seen before or since, was remarkably sensitive to what was going on, not only in my unconscious but between my supervisor and myself as we discussed this patient's treatment on a weekly basis.

When I first saw Hyman Cohen in consultation I immediately liked him. He was fifty, about five feet, ten inches and solidly built, with a pleasant face and appealing manner. Born in Russia, he spoke with a heavy accent and had no education beyond the eighth grade. But despite his lack of education, he was a voracious reader, a well-read Marxist who had learned much about psychoanalysis and had devoured Freud.

He worked in the garment industry, and his wife was office manager in a cosmetics firm. He sought analysis because he had several psychosomatic problems, including asthma, migraine headaches, and ulcers. He admitted he felt anxious on his job and had strong feelings of inferiority because of his lack of education. He was also having sexual problems in his marriage, and frequent obsessions, largely centering on food.

I found him likable, and his wish to improve himself, despite his lack of formal education, endeared him to me further. He described his mother as a depressed woman who probably was schizophrenic. His father, who died when Hyman was nine, also sounded like an extremely disturbed man.

Hyman was referred by a colleague who was treating Hyman's wife. She could not stand his crude ways of approaching her sexually, his constant phobias regarding food, his long political sermons, and his lack of sophistication.

During the first therapy sessions I decided this difficult, complicated case would need intensive supervision. After seeing Hyman three times, I made arrangements to consult Marie Coleman Nelson on a weekly basis as my supervisor. Hyman's session usually followed the supervisory session by one day.

My description of this case is drawn from the copious notes I took on Hyman's case. Each therapy hour discussed below follows the supervisory hour summarized above it. In every instance, though I had made no reference in Hyman's therapy to the content of the supervisory hour, he habitually showed an ability to somehow relate to what Marie and I had talked about the previous day. I should point out that his therapy was not classical psychoanalysis but a modified form of supportive psychotherapy.

After arranging my first appointment with Marie, though I had not yet seen her, I entered my office for Hyman's session. He promptly stated, "I was very dissatisfied with you after the last time. I thought of quitting. I was not optimistic about the future. But now I have more confidence in you. *You* look more confident today. Maybe you've made an appointment to see *your* analyst."

Somehow he knew or sensed I had arranged an appointment designed to help me help him. I never told him I was consulting a supervisor or of the supervisory sessions. There follows a sample account of the supervisory session, then his session a day later.

Supervisory session no. 1: When I met Marie for our first

session we discussed Hyman's history and current problems. Then we tried to make a comprehensive diagnosis. She asked if I had brought in process notes so we could examine a therapy hour in detail. I said I did not have a recording of a therapeutic hour with Hyman nor had I taken notes, but I would see she had ample material in a week or two. Approximately one hour after this meeting, a colleague asked me how the supervision went. I replied, "She relates to me like a peer. I like her. She gave me a lot."

Marie and I discussed Hyman's continual preoccupation with food. She pointed out that I should not try to interpret this obsession because it protected him against strong oral sadism that was frightening to him. She said, "You might try to read about food and talk to him about it, giving him permission to have the food obsession." In other words, Marie was saying that only after Hyman felt I had given him permission to obsess about food would he think of giving it up.

Before my next session with Hyman I read an article called "Foods, Fads and Fancies," and consciously thought of Hyman as I read it.

Therapy session (the following day): Hyman started this session by saying, "I have just read an interesting article called 'Foods, Fads and Fancies,' but this diet business is too much for me. I think about it too much, and I want to give it up."

Supervisory session no. 11: Marie told me that my interpreting part of the homosexual transference that Hyman had shown in a dream was premature. She said it stimulated too much anxiety in him, reminded him of a psychiatrist he had seen many years before, who focused on homosexuality. This had provoked Hyman to leave the treatment. Marie suggested it might be helpful to Hyman and the therapy if I told Hyman I had erred.

Therapy session (a day later): Hyman entered and said, "I had sexual relations with my wife and it got me very anxious. I had a premature ejaculation. All that stuff about me loving you didn't help me. You reminded me of Dr. Smith whom I left a year ago. I think you made a mistake."

Supervisory session no. 19: I told Marie I was impressed with Hyman's strong murderous fantasies beneath his obsessive defense. After some discussion, she said, "Maybe you should ask him cheerfully when he plans to murder you. Play that game. I think he'll like it."

Therapy session (one day later): Hyman reported a dream: "I was playing cops and robbers with you. It was a murder game but fun."

Supervisory session no. 27: Marie noted that Hyman "never stays with one topic but flits all over the place." She added, "It might be helpful to bring him back to the topic and see what he does when you show him this."

Therapy session (a day later): Hyman started this session with a resumé of events at his job. He rambled on from one topic to another, and just as I was ready to intervene, he said, "I'll have to watch myself if you don't watch me. I should tell you the whole thing and stick to it instead of going all over the place."

Supervisory session no. 49: Marie and I discussed the fact that Hyman fantasied me as the mother he always wanted. Furthermore, we agreed he seemed to be asking for something from me. She said, "Perhaps it would be a remedial experience to help him with this." Because he had been making many references to clothes and his concern about his appearance, she suggested, "Why don't you see what happens when you offer him some help in choosing the proper clothes?"

Therapy session (a day later): Hyman said his wife had called him a slob. He remembered being referred to, as a child and while growing up, as the black sheep of the family because he "never wore the proper clothes." He then suggested to me, "Maybe you can help me with this."

Supervisory session no. 52: Marie and I agreed that, since Hyman was now coming to the sessions in new clothes, he was simply acting out a wish to comply with me, like a submissive child; it was not a genuine working through of the conflict. She said, "He should be kept guessing as to what your stand on clothes is. Question him as to why he now comes all dressed up to the sessions."

Therapy session (a day later): Hyman entered my office dressed sloppily once more. He said, "I don't see why I should listen to you about getting all dressed up. I want to be free, not a conformist."

Supervisory session no. 59: Marie and I noted Hyman had been making progress in therapy. His marriage, particularly his sexual relationship, his work problems, and his social adjustment all had improved. Marie remarked, "He talks as if he's cured. It might be a good idea to explore how he feels about terminating. Not that he's ready to, but let's see what he does with the idea."

Therapy session (a day later): Hyman entered the office looking pale. He lay down on the couch and moaned, "Every problem I had has come back. I feel very bad. My job gets me anxious. My wife is always yelling at me. And I feel uncomfortable with people again. Do you think this analysis will ever end?"

Supervisory session no. 66: I discussed with Marie the continual preoccupation Hyman had with noise. She quipped, "A noisy noise annoys an oyster."

Therapy session (one day later): Hyman began by complaining, "Before I came here I had supper at Paddy's. I was eating oysters. The place was so noisy. Now, was that annoying!"

I could give other dramatic evidence of Hyman's unconscious awareness of specific, identifiable events occurring in my private sessions with my supervisor. The question that still confronts me about this case is how he was able to unconsciously perceive what was going on in these discussions.

Though I worked with Hyman almost thirty years ago, I

am still not sure what made him so attuned to my thoughts, particularly in those supervisory hours. No definite conclusion seems satisfactory, even after thirty years. But I would like to suggest some hypotheses.

My first hypothesis is that Hyman and I were psychologically similar. He yearned for the understanding and care of a parental figure, and this has been a powerful wish in me. Somehow I must have showed him in my tone, movements, and speech that I had yearnings to be fed that matched his dietary obsessions and that we were therefore like brothers under the skin. Perhaps when one person is highly sensitive to another person's unconscious, the unconscious wishes and fantasies of the two may be very similar.

A second hypothesis evolves from Hyman's history. He never perceived his parents relating to each other as a couple. He consistently described his mother as deficient in nurturing and his father as inadequate as an object for masculine identification. Perhaps his dream of seeing me with a woman could be interpreted as a wish for two parents. It is even conceivable he unconsciously induced me to secure a female supervisor so at last he received what he had always craved—two parents relating and working together in his behalf. Perhaps he felt more secure as he sensed me interacting with a woman because of his unhappiness.

There was no doubt Hyman's enthusiasm for and involvement in therapy lessened after I ended the supervision. I have also wondered whether I became less enthusiastic without Marie in the picture.

I know that when Hyman ended therapy he functioned much more adequately. But it is still an open question as to how much of this occurred because he sensed I was talking about him with a maternal figure, the fulfillment of his fantasy.

I believe one of the most important factors in understanding Hyman's ability to anticipate my therapeutic interventions was his sensing my involvement with another therapist.

181

With Marie I endeavored to be the perfect son who gives his mother precisely what she wants. Early in my work with her, I knew she felt truly gratified when I reported Hyman's anticipation of what I was going to say, always derived from the supervisory hour.

And just as I received gratification in loving and being loved by Marie, I believe Hyman wished for this kind of relationship not only from me, whom he experienced most of the time as a father figure, but also from a mother figure. He was a somewhat sophisticated man who knew how psychoanalysts are trained, and he might have had some preconscious awareness that I was in supervision with a woman analyst. His first dream, in which he pictured me being fed by a woman after which I fed him, followed my calling Marie for supervision. The dream pointed to his strong wish to visualize me talking about him with a woman. He could then see himself as the recipient of maternal and paternal concern in a way he had never known as a child.

I have often reflected on this unique case, one unlike any other before or after in the many years I have practiced psychoanalysis. I believe my strong symbiotic wishes for a parental figure were gratified in my supervisory hours with Marie and this gratification was somehow transmitted to Hyman. I said at the start of this chapter that an analyst uses his unconscious to get in touch with the patient's unconscious, and I think Hyman used his unconscious to get in touch with my unconscious.

His yearnings for a symbiotic relationship with a parent or parents mirrored my own. He and I were like symbiotic twins. (It occurred to me just now that the name I unconsciously selected to use for this patient is my own Hebrew name. This shows I still feel, decades later, a strong identification with Hyman.)

Marie and I often discussed in the supervisory meetings the fact that despite Hyman's lack of formal education, there was something "great and brilliant" about him. We even conjectured that had he undergone a formal education he might have turned out to be a brilliant psychoanalyst or statesman.

I recall, after a conversation with Marie in which we talked of Hyman's potential, I realized how much I had yearned to have two parents talk about my potential as a youth. As I analyzed this wish, I recalled the time I was eight and overheard my mother tell my father what a provocative boy I was, constantly giving her a hard time. My father sounded helpless, though concerned, as he listened to my mother's angry complaints. How deeply I wished, as I overheard that conversation, to have parents who spoke as Marie and I did when we talked about Hyman, wanting only to help him live a happier life.

The day after one rather prolonged discussion in which Marie and I discussed Hyman's "greatness," he told me he had just seen the movie *The Hucksters*. "There was a character in it who had a quality of greatness and brilliance," he said. "I identified with this man and thought it would be wonderful to be like him."

Perhaps Hyman did achieve a quality of greatness, not only by resolving many of his conflicts but by showing an unconscious sensitivity to an analyst's thoughts.

Though many of Hyman's statements may be attributed to coincidence or may sound like magic, I believe there were too many instances in too many analytic hours where he repeated almost word for word what Marie and I had said, to attribute it all to chance. We believe that the analyst uses his unconscious to sensitize himself to his patient's unconscious. Why should we not accept that a patient may be attuned to his analyst's unconscious?

Theodor Reik pointed out that analysts listen to patients with a "third ear." We should not deprive Hyman, or any other analytic patient, of also possessing a "third ear."

I believe that perhaps there are other Hymans in other psychoanalytic practices, but they are not reported by practitioners. I learned from Hyman early in my professional career that patients can have a better functioning "third ear" than their analysts—at least some of the time. It took me years to really "digest" this notion which, at first, felt quite threatening to me. However, if psychoanalysts truly want to be empathic human beings, they should learn to accept that their patients can be as attuned to their unconscious as analysts try to be with their patients.

11

A FAILURE
The Professor Who
Successfully Defeated Me

Professor Albert Weiss, thirty-six years old, walked into the consultation room a number of years ago. He was chunky but solid, with a strong, chiseled face, and looked more like a successful football player than a philosophy professor.

As soon as he spoke, I knew I was in trouble. Most patients who seek analytic help have an air of reticence, acknowledge their discomfort, and show a certain amount of deference to me. But Professor Weiss, after seating himself, belligerently demanded, "What are your credentials?"

While many patients do ask for my credentials, it is the rare person who asks in such a demeaning way. I felt irritated and defensive. I wanted to say, "What's it to you?"

Though I remained calm, my voice sounded irritated, defensive, and challenging as I said, "Could you tell me what your concern is about my credentials?"

He then said, in the same provocative tone, "I'm not sure you're qualified to help me. That's why I need to know your credentials."

Again I felt like a boxer in a ring, overpowered by a larger man, cringing, vulnerable, ready to run, escape—an unusual feeling for me, but one I do experience on rare occasions, as I did with this patient and with Robert Nelson, whom I spoke of in Chapter 8.

Albert Weiss proceeded to hammer away at me. He said pompously, "I have a feeling you are reluctant to talk about yourself."

Clearly, he was trying to put me in the patient's seat, force me to reveal myself to him. Partly because I sensed this attempt, but also to protect myself, I said, in a voice probably an octave higher than my normal one, "I think you would like to analyze me and find out all about my life without telling me anything about yourself."

To my surprise Albert simmered down. He actually half smiled. "You're not a complete patsy, are you? When I first looked at you I thought you were an effeminate patsy, but you can hit back."

Not very professional words, I thought, but I was glad his remarks sounded somewhat reassuring. In many ways I did feel a bit overpowered by him, and when he told me I wasn't a patsy I felt better. Maybe he *was* doing therapy, since my anxiety did diminish—while I got paid for it, incidentally.

Usually after a first interview, I feel an eager and interested anticipation of the next session, much like the feeling of getting ready to go on a journey. This time, however, I found myself obsessing about Albert after he left. I knew from my analytic training that obsessing is a sign of mixed feelings.

After my first interview with Albert, and after a number of succeeding sessions, I engaged in fantasied arguments in which I was trying to ward off a bully who made me feel weak and vulnerable. Obviously Albert threatened me and it was difficult for me to acknowledge this truth, so I argued with him in fantasy. In hindsight, I have to admit my work with him was a failure in that I could not give him the help he was entitled to receive and was, I believe, capable of using.

I should mention that the subject of the analyst's failure is not sufficiently considered in the psychoanalytic literature. Though Freud made use of case presentations in his writings, in only one or two of his cases does he talk of his own failure with the patient. One example is the early case of Dora, described in *Freud and Women*, which Lucy Freeman and I wrote. Dora was an eighteen-year-old girl who left treatment prematurely. Freud later said he did not sufficiently consider Dora's sexual transference toward him. But contemporary psychoanalysts say Freud also did not consider his erotic feelings toward Dora. Perhaps he let his conflicts interfere with the success of the case, causing her to leave him abruptly.

Psychoanalysts say that in trying to understand behavior and attitudes there are no saints and no sinners. But when analysts look at cases that fail they tend to ascribe the failure to the patient's "poor motivation," "negative transference," and "inability to face certain material such as hostile or sexual thoughts." However, after years of reviewing my own work and the work of colleagues and students, I believe it is equally possible in cases that fail for the analyst to be poorly motivated. He may have negative feelings toward the patient, or he may fail to acknowledge certain of his own attitudes.

In cases that ended prematurely or in which patients returned with problems that were clearly not well analyzed, I have often found in hindsight that the issues about which the patient needed help and did not receive it were issues I was resisting in myself. I believe this was true in the case of Albert, whom I treated in the late 1960s, and I have found it true in other cases where I was not successful.

I believe that when the material from the patient stirs up unresolved conflicts in the analyst, he is not in a position to be helpful in a meaningful way. In the past ten years or so my failures have been much less frequent, primarily because I am reaping the benefits of a successful personal analysis, which also helps me to do effective self-analysis as I observe myself with my patients.

After Albert concluded I was not a complete patsy, he started to tell me about his problems. He was caught, he said, in a severe marital conflict. He and his wife had daily arguments during which he sometimes became violent and pushed her or threw her on the floor. I suspect there were even more violent episodes, which he hid from me. The couple had a four-year-old son.

Their arguments, according to Albert, arose from the difference in their personalities. He described himself as a logical (as befits a professor of philosophy), responsible, well-organized man, whereas his wife, as he perceived her, was a frivolous, disorganized, overly romantic woman who easily gave way to tears and was "much too anxious." Analysts would describe this marriage as the classical alliance between the cold, obsessive-compulsive husband and the hysterical wife. Albert took almost no responsibility for the marital conflicts and was not sure why he had entered therapy, inasmuch as he saw himself almost exclusively as a "victim of circumstance."

I asked, "How do you think we can use our time here?"

He responded like the philosophy professor he was. "I thought if I told you about the marriage, you might be able to help me understand my wife's psychopathology."

It is not the purpose of analysis to help a patient understand someone else—it is difficult enough to help him understand himself—yet sometimes the understanding of others is a by-product. But I respected Albert's *modus operandi*, realizing he was protecting himself against looking at his own neurotic conflicts. In time the courage to examine himself would slowly emerge.

But I felt within myself once again a deep annoyance at Albert. Here I was, a young, married man with a child, and also a budding professor, trying my best to see how I could improve as husband and father, and here was Albert, in my mind getting away with murder.

I realized quite early in my work with him that I was jealous. I had to try with all my heart and mind to understand myself in my marriage and in my work. Albert could blame others and escape the difficult task I faced. On some level I am sure he felt some need for help—otherwise he would not have come to me—but he defended strongly against it with his arrogance. I was responding not so much to his need but to his arrogance.

At the time I worked with Albert I did not recognize how competitive I felt and how threatened I was in his presence. If I had, I would not have felt the continual power struggle in which I was involved, both in and out of treatment.

Something happened in my work with Albert that I believe occurs in many analytic encounters: I often said the correct words, but my attitude and tone were frequently hostile and defensive. When I read and study an analyst's case studies and interpretations, I notice something that is often missing from the reports: his feelings as he makes his interpretations. Did he speak the words seductively, provocatively, angrily? The analyst's tone may be more important than his words.

During my early sessions with Albert I told him, correctly, "You have doubts about me." But my words did not hold the warm, empathic tone they did when I spoke the same words to other patients.

In the "here and now" of my work with Professor Albert Weiss, I was involved in a competitive duel. He was a formidable opponent who told me scornfully I did not know my business well, and I wanted to show him otherwise. I also wanted to exert some power over him and force him to admit his frailties. I could justify this by making all kinds of "analytic interpretations," but clearly I was making Albert my father of the past, who also had seemed so much bigger and stronger than I. I wanted to show him I was just as strong as he.

The greatest difficulty for me was that I could not monitor my feelings enough to help him analytically, even though I was sometimes conscious of my difficulties with him. I knew I was distorting Albert, making him a Goliath while I felt like a David. I needed more personal analysis to rise "above the battle." Unfortunately, my wish to "beat out the old man" was stronger than my wish to help Albert.

Though I did not tell Albert my credentials, he learned them. He then demeaned the school where I trained and said I was "probably a little less than average" as analysts went. I listened to his criticisms and consciously tried to help him see that he wanted to fight, but within myself I fought as actively as he did, trying to show him I was not as small or "castrated" as he perceived me.

Even when I kept quiet and let him attack me verbally, I felt my silence was not a therapeutic silence but an angry one. I did not respond with support or understanding because I felt too intimidated by this overpowering professor who, on some level, I felt was too much for me, just as I had felt my father was too much for me when I was a little boy.

In another dimension of my work with Albert I found myself again responding defensively. He frequently, as I mentioned, seemed to want to analyze me. He told me my interest in being quiet and investigating his unconscious was an attempt on my part to gain power.

"You only want to control me," he charged. "You're afraid I will be more powerful than you."

While this statement could be viewed as projection of his wish for power, it was nevertheless an accurate assessment of my feelings toward him. And because I was aware of the correctness of his evaluations, I could not relax sufficiently to help him examine his struggles and conflicts.

Actually my work with him should not really be called psychoanalytic treatment. It was more of an interpersonal struggle between two men who felt uncomfortable with each other, each one trying to prove his potency to the other and to himself.

Albert's background was somewhat similar to mine. He had an authoritarian father; so did I. His mother preferred his younger sister; so did mine. He was conflicted about whether to be a strong man for father or an effeminate boy for mother; so was I.

I think that Albert and I saw in each other qualities we did not like in ourselves. It was as though we both looked into a mirror, shuddered, and said, "Oh, what a terrible sight!"

While I have focused on my countertransference problems with Albert, there were times I worked with him objectively, feeling less involved in a power struggle. When this occurred, he became less hostile. After ten months of treatment he moved into a positive phase. He started to feel warmly toward me.

This feeling of warmth, however, made him uncomfortable because it stirred up wishes to be a young girl with a mother, and this made him feel upset about homosexual fantasies. A fascinating but understandable occurrence took place after a year of treatment. Albert went to concerts once a week. After one concert he said to me, "You were there sitting next to me, enjoying the concert with me."

His conviction that I was present was so strong that I had to assume he'd experienced a hallucination. He'd obviously had a deep wish for me to be there with him listening to classical music. Later on, he became paranoid, and insisted I was following him on the street. His paranoid charges were so strong and so hostile that again I was unable to be sufficiently sensitive to his fear of closeness. Instead of encouraging him to associate to his feelings about being at the concert with me, I said not a word, sat in reciprocally hostile silence.

One more time my feeling of being intimidated interfered with my analytic work. Instead of helping Albert explore his fantasy of sitting next to me at Carnegie Hall, instead of helping him recognize the part of him that wished to be a child with me, I interpreted prematurely his wish to sit next to me at a concert: He wanted me to be a lover, to make sweet music with him.

My interpretation could almost have been justified except it was an attempt to stop him from attacking me, and I am sure my tone reflected my discomfort. I was uncomfortable with the closeness he was suggesting. His latent homosexual wish stirred up something similar in me, and I became the cold, objective analyst rather than the empathic one. To be empathic would have made me feel like a lover on a date with Albert, listening to music together.

My premature interpretation made him become more paranoid. He then experienced me as a rejecting analyst. His relationship to his wife worsened; he turned more violent and hostile.

I have said elsewhere that when the marriage of a patient who is in analysis takes a turn for the worse, the feelings the patient expresses toward his wife are really directed at the analyst. For many years now I have been sensitive to the fact that when the patient goes on a rampage with a spouse, child, colleague, employer, or friend, he is really displacing feelings toward me. I did not understand this with Albert, however, because I was defending myself too strongly against him, and I might even have derived some satisfaction from seeing him fail in his marriage.

Eventually Albert's marriage broke up, and their son went to live with his mother. Albert said to me confidently, "I'm better off alone, without her and the boy. I really do better as a a loner."

He then became a Don Juan, filled his sessions with bragging about his "sexual exploits" with one woman after another. He appeared euphoric at times, grandiose. He said to me, "I'm much happier now. No one around to drive me crazy with her craziness. Now I can see more appropriate women and spend time enhancing myself professionally."

He added a taunt: "In every respect, my life is better than yours, I am sure."

He found out I was an assistant professor and boasted that he was an associate professor. He learned I wrote articles and sniffed, "I've written far more articles than you have." The final taunt: "I'm sure you're a patsy in bed with your wife. I'm out having exciting sex with any woman I choose."

When Albert left treatment after two years, he was in the same emotional state as when he first arrived—perhaps slightly worse. His arrogance in some ways seemed stronger. His tenderness and capacity to love seemed diminished, in spite of his insistence that he was a capable seducer (tenderness and love have little to do with seduction). His willingness to face himself was virtually nil.

Though Albert derived very little, if any benefit from the treatment, I learned a great deal. Many of my mistakes with him have been helpful to me when other patients have tried to involve me in a power struggle. I have learned, for example, that when a patient wants to turn the analysis into a tug-of-war, he is feeling vulnerable and weak and that if I respond with anything but empathy and understanding *I* am feeling vulnerable and weak.

What is important for the analyst is important for the patient—he wants to be a child but feels uncomfortable about the wish. In hindsight, I wanted to make Albert my father and be his son, and I hated myself for it. But instead of fully examining my countertransference, as I would today, I defended against it with big-shot interpretations rather than empathic observations.

One might ask why I lost my objectivity with Albert rather than with some other patient. I believe there were several reasons. The most obvious is that I was not sufficiently well analyzed at that point and tended to protect myself too readily. But I believe the major reason for my failure with Albert was that we were very similar in certain ways and I did not want to face this in myself.

Albert's conflicts when he first walked into my office were conflicts of my own which I had not as yet sufficiently faced or mastered. Albert had unresolved wishes to be his sister, as did I. Albert coped with his passive wishes by being pseudoaggressive, as I did. Albert, despite his many strengths, wished to be a little child, and so did I at times. Albert needed more understanding and a more analytic attitude from a helper. So did I.

I have often wondered what happened to Albert. I hope he eventually found someone who could help him more effectively.

12

ANALYZING AN AUTISTIC CHILD
The Boy Who Called
Me a Machine

Adam Blaine was a slight, handsome six-year-old boy with large gray-blue eyes, brown hair, and a very depressed look. He walked into my waiting room one day in the late 1960s accompanied by his mother, a worried-looking woman in her early thirties, with straight dark hair drawn severely back from her face.

Adam was immaculately dressed as was his mother, Mary Blaine, who had described herself over the phone as "a budding artist." She was married to Arthur Blaine, an archeologist on the staff of a Manhattan museum.

As I entered the waiting room to greet him and his mother, Adam looked away from me. I led him into my office, after telling his mother we would be out in forty-five minutes. Adam continued to avoid my eyes as we sat opposite each other in the office. He kept his body stiff, looked like a robot. This rigid position continued for several weeks.

As I tried to make eye contact with Adam in the first session and succeeding interviews, I sensed his strong wish to be left alone in whatever world he occupied. He opposed anything resembling a human relationship.

Prior to meeting Adam, I had seen both his father and mother to get a full description of his problems and as comprehensive a history as they could furnish. Both parents, in separate and joint interviews, told me Adam rarely talked. A complete set of neurological examinations and other tests had ruled out any physical causes for his silence. Though his IQ was 130, he appeared to his teachers at times to be an imbecile. Everyone thought, to use his parents' word, he looked "peculiar."

Adam had two younger brothers who, according to the parents, were easy to manage, likable, and spontaneous. In comparison they called Adam an "oddball." He had no friends and seemed interested only in playing with his erector set and other mechanical games.

When I heard about Adam's behavior from his parents, I suspected he was an autistic child. Autism implies exclusive preoccupation with the self, little if any ability to show interest in others.

There is to this day great debate about the cause of autism. A number of prominent child therapists and psychoanalysts believe the cause is constitutional and/or organic. Others believe the autistic child is too terrified to engage in contact with anyone. They maintain the infant from birth on is a social being and the term "autistic schizophrenia" describes a child who basically remains an infant so emotionally stunted he cannot develop normally.

Those professionals who consider autism organic or constitutional decry psychotherapy as a treatment. Those who believe autism is a result of a child's relationship with his mother and father champion psychotherapy for both child and parents. While I think the constitutional and physical causes of any emotional problem should never be dismissed,

I feel that some children's autism grows out of emotional experiences with their parents. I felt that Adam was one of these children.

It has been my experience that many autistic children have lived with what I call "refrigerated parents." Adam's mother and father were typical refrigerated parents. They were both very intelligent and knowledgeable but emotionally detached. Like other parents of autistic children, they arrived at the interviews with reams of notes, presenting as accurate a chronology of a child's development as one could hope to find.

As I listened to Adam's parents describe what they called his "psychosocial development," it did not take me long to sense they were frightened of expressing love and tenderness to this child. They went through the motions of child-rearing but neither could have shown much warmth, caring, or elation during their six years with Adam.

Yet, as they spoke of their two younger sons, they displayed animation and love. I felt puzzled by this at first, and I am sure this disparity has contributed to the controversy raging among professionals regarding the origins of autistic schizophrenia. If Adam's parents could show love toward his two younger brothers, it was easy to argue that Adam, from birth on, was suffering organic and constitutional problems and was therefore difficult to reach. Certainly his parents had the capacity to love their two younger children. So the argument for nonpsychological causes could be made in diagnosing Adam.

But as I learned more about the parents, I discounted more and more the constitutional and organic factors in Adam. Some glaring revelations about both parents led to my belief that much of Adam's difficulties had to do with the unresolved problems of the parents.

What were some of these parental problems? Both were the oldest children in their own natural families. Both described their parents as "cold, intellectual, and unable to play." As I explored with them in depth their own childhoods, it became clear that, as children, they had been emotionally neglected, unloved. They had strong dependency yearnings against which they'd had to erect defenses. As Mary and Arthur grew up, they were loved more by their parents. They emerged in later life with some capacity to give and take.

Dr. Margaret Mahler has referred to the first three months of life as the "autistic stage," when the infant is almost exclusively preoccupied with his own bodily needs and sensations. I believed Adam's difficulty had occurred primarily in these first few months of life—the stage Mahler calls "autistic." Parents who have not been cuddled tenderly and fussed over as babies cannot offer love to their children. They defend against acknowledging their early yearnings, reenact what was done unto them with the child who reminds them the most of themselves. Adam, like both of his parents, was the firstborn. Mary and Arthur were terrified of his infantile wishes for love, attention, tenderness, which reminded them of their early years. Imitating their parents, which all of us do when it comes to displaying love, Mary and Arthur loved their younger sons more than their firstborn.

Both parents came to me on a weekly basis, and I worked to help them get in touch with the "Adam" in themselves. They slowly became more loving, much less "refrigerated" parents. I am certain their emotional growth was an important element in Adam's eventual change.

I saw him three times a week for three years. The treatment was difficult, and many times I felt discouraged. I had worked with autistic children in treatment camps and other settings, but Adam was the first autistic child I treated in analysis.

If persistence were not my middle name I would have given up on Adam after several months of sheer analytic drudgery. Following a few sessions in which Adam just stared at the ceiling, I tried my first intervention.

"I know you don't want to have much to do with me, Adam," I said. "Being here makes you very uncomfortable, doesn't it?"

He kept his silence. I could only conclude my words had made him feel more uncomfortable. He gazed with even more rigidity at the ceiling, creating a greater distance between us.

I said, after a few more minutes of silence, "What I just said made you angry at me."

With that he turned his body firmly away from me. It was then the full meaning of "autism" became imprinted on my mind: not a word, no communication—not from the eyes or the lips. Nothing.

I had worked with withdrawn children before, children who opposed me, did not wish to notice me or want me to notice them. But Adam had a quality that seemed to say, "I am a block of ice. I refuse to melt. I want nothing to do with you."

My feelings during the first several weeks were mixed. I felt challenged and excited on the one hand, irritated by Adam's powerful resistance on the other. I think he sensed I was trying to get close to him, and was determined to defeat all my attempts.

During the second and third months he literally built a wall between us as he worked with wooden blocks. But at least he now moved from the chair to the floor to play with the blocks. He built his block-walls so high I could not see him. Other children usually used the blocks to construct houses or shacks, but Adam used them to block me out of his life and to block himself out of mine.

Adam's wish to block me out affected me deeply. I thought of him after work on many occasions and once or twice relished my sons' responsiveness to me, reassuring myself I was not such an ogre after all.

As I coped with his rejection—a rejection more profound than any I ever experienced from a patient, child or adult, before or since—I realized my wish to involve Adam in a relationship was compounding his resistance to me. I thought he was like an angry virgin who warned, "Stay away from me. I don't want anything to do with you," as I pleaded, "Please, please, open up to me."

As I became more in touch with my untherapeutic need for involvement, I began to identify more with Adam. I thought of the times as a child when I wanted to build walls, realized they occurred when I felt an impotent fury I feared to express. In the first months of Adam's treatment I had failed to attune myself to the powerful murderous rage his withdrawal and lack of communication defended against. As soon as I sensed this rage in him, his therapy began to move a bit better.

One day as he built a wall of blocks to keep me out of sight, I decided *I* would build a wall to keep *him* out of sight. As I piled my blocks higher and higher, Adam smiled—his first smile.

Then he spoke his first words. "You want to play war?"

Delighted at this communication, aggressive though it was, I said overzealously, "Sure."

He said not another word that day. But at the next session he announced, as he built his wall of blocks, "I'm a Nazi. I'll kill you. You are a stupid machine."

"What's stupid about me?" I asked.

He said contemptuously, "You don't know *anything*."

In subsequent sessions I realized that "stupid machine" was actually Adam's image for his mother and father, as they appeared to him early in life. At that time they did not know much about giving a child love and care; they were incapable of truly loving their first child because he brought back painful memories of their infancy. They related to him like machines, in a robotlike way. Adam related to them as they did to him. He became a machine, incapable of love, even as he yearned desperately for it.

I now knew he hid an explosive rage. A rage he feared would blow up the universe if he showed it. It was safer to be autistic than to express such a rage.

I realized Adam needed to view me as a machine, as he viewed everyone else. By stopping me from expressing warm human feelings he could stop himself from having such feelings toward me. Yet by angrily berating me by calling me a machine, Adam showed he was giving up some of his robotlike qualities and embarking on his first human relationship, albeit very tentatively and angrily.

I was pleased Adam at least now talked to me, as demeaning and hypercritical as he was. This meant he was no longer the automaton he had appeared to be when we first met. By viewing me as a machine, Adam projected his self-image onto me. Because his hatred of me was essentially self-hatred, as well as hatred of his unfeeling parents, I felt that by asking him how I, the machine, worked, I would further understand Adam and help him understand the emotions against which he was defending himself.

For one thing, I thought, when you are a small, unloved child and see your parents giving all their love to two newcomers, your jealousy and envy will be so acute you might well become mute out of fear of expressing your rage in wild cries of reproach, as though to scream, "I'm here, too."

One day Adam paid me a great compliment for a change: "You're a thinking machine." For the first time in the eight months I had known him, he laughed. He then said, "You think funny thoughts. You think of throwing doody at the world and turning the doody into bombs." He added, "You're a doody-head."

As I explored with him what he thought I was angry about, he informed me I wanted to throw "doody" at the world because the world threw "doody" at me. I knew Adam was talking about himself, saying he'd "taken a lot of shit" and wanted to hurl it back at anyone and everyone.

I felt extremely compassionate with Adam at this point. I could identify with his fury as I thought of the many times I wanted to cover my parents and other hostile parental figures with fecal matter. But I also realized I had to go easy in interpreting his rage because I knew he would not have walled it off for so long unless it was terrifying.

I tentatively suggested, "I guess I want to throw doody at the world because the world has thrown doody at me. Maybe you've felt that happened to you."

For the first time in treatment, perhaps in his life, Adam revealed he felt understood by asking me to be his ally. He said, "You and I should throw doody at the whole world because the world hates us." The "whole world," for Adam, was his parents—parents are every child's whole world.

Adam then showed me that I had earned his trust by speaking about his younger brothers: "I know my mother and father like Eddie and Robby better than me. No one was ever real nice to me." He added, "You know what that feels like, Mr. Machine, because it happened to you, too"— and in many ways, he was right. He stared at me earnestly, as though asking me to be his friend.

I felt happy he was now able to speak of his feelings. I was convinced his autism represented a powerful defense against murderous feelings. The more I could help him talk about his fury and fantasies—or about mine, since mine were a projection of his—the more he would gain a sense of his own identity.

Slowly Adam relaxed with me, and the wall between us began to tumble down. He smiled more often, he entered my office and greeted me with enthusiasm. Then one day he began to regress, started to talk like a baby, which he had never dared do.

I was prepared for this. In my work with other very disturbed children—adults, too, for that matter—I had learned that the more they felt understood and empathized with, the freer they felt to express the primitive child within.

The first few times I saw open, regressive behavior in a child or adult, I was frightened. I thought they were going crazy in front of my eyes, I felt powerless to rescue them. But as I studied my feelings of impotence and reflected more on my patient's state of mind while he regressed, I realized that what the psychoanalyst Heinz Hartmann referred to as "regression in the service of the ego" could be therapeutic. Most psychological difficulties arise because we rigorously defend ourselves against regressive childish wishes. As those childish wishes become more acceptable to us, we feel a sense of freedom, as though a psychic burden had been lifted from our frail shoulders. We no longer need to use psychic energy to repress the childish wishes and fantasies.

And so I felt encouraged as Adam moved toward baby talk, then started to crawl, reenacting his early development. He was becoming the baby he always wanted to be and could not because he was forbidden emotionally from birth on to be a spontaneous baby who cried when he felt hurt or in need, who wanted to be held tenderly. In his early years, his emotional spontaneity had terrified his mother and father.

Because Adam needed the experience of being a baby with a loving parent, I talked baby talk with him. We played games together in which we pretended he was my baby and I was either his daddy or his mommy. I had overcome my fear of the kind of regression I observed in Adam. In the past I had worried whether this regression would be carried over into the rest of the patient's life, that the child or adult would act like a baby outside the office. It took this experience with Adam to show me my worry was unfounded.

When a child or adult is given permission to reveal the emotionally hungry infant inside, he invariably functions much better on the outside. This happened to Adam. He became more alert, more emotionally responsive, much less autistic.

Both parents progressed, too. They each needed to speak of their deep yearnings, profound emotional hunger, and wish for love. They became more giving with Adam. He in turn was ready to receive their love, forgive their "machine-like" quality during his earliest years.

Then I made a glaring mistake with Adam. My excitement at seeing an autistic, robotlike child emerge into a spontaneous child threatened him. As I spoke baby talk, smiled at him, and giggled with him, he started again to withdraw, return to a more mechanical way of relating.

At first I was unaware I was inducing Adam to become more machinelike. I thought he was just frightened of feeling emotions that had terrified him in the past. Although this was true, I could sense after a while that my enthusiasm made him experience me as an engulfing mother.

This was a mistake I had made in the past with children and sometimes with adults, too—I showed my pleasure at their progress, my eagerness to help them. Some patients flourish under such circumstances, but those with doubts and insecurities about close relationships become frightened and suspicious. When I was twenty and a counselor at a camp for disturbed youngsters, one of my campers was walking into the swimming pool and I said spontaneously, "Attaboy, Sunny." He wheeled around, said to me skeptically, "I haven't done anything yet. Why are you praising me?"

Now, more than two decades later, the same situation occurred with Adam. I was not sufficiently tempering my enthusiasm, and this frightened Adam. I had to monitor this behavior and would probably have to do so for the rest of my therapeutic life. I suspect the major reason I get excited when my patients progress is that I so identify with them I become the parental figure I always wanted. Once in my personal analysis I remarked to my analyst, "If someone gives me a gumdrop, I soar"—implying if anyone responds to me in the least degree, I feel as if I'm walking on air. The word "gumdrop" related to the joy I felt when my grandmother served me delicious food and sweets along with warm compliments. Grandmothers, by the way, may be very important in a child's life; I suspect it's no accident they came to be called "grand mothers."

I realized Adam was frightened by my excitement at his progress. I said to him, "I am sorry if I scared you because I felt you were coming along so well."

Though he did not forgive me quickly, he clearly felt more at ease when he realized I understood what I had done that made him feel endangered.

Whenever it is clear I have said or done something that interferes with analytic work, I find it helpful to share this with the patient. He feels less alone in his misery, more understood by a parental figure. He realizes it is not so crucial to have an omnipotent parent, that if his analyst can make mistakes so can he.

Once when I told an adolescent I was wrong in interpreting something prematurely, he remarked, showing insight, "I guess that's why pencils have erasers."

One reason hearing an analyst say he has made a mistake proves therapeutic for most patients is that few of us in growing up ever hear our parents admit they have made a mistake or been wrong in any way. I never heard my mother or father once say they had erred, and I vowed that as parent or therapist I would not do the same thing. When I am convinced I have made an incorrect interpretation and it has had a detrimental effect, I find it is helpful both to the patient and to me to acknowledge the truth. Tensions diminish and relationships improve when the parental figure admits the truth about his own limitations and the possibility of human error.

When Adam realized I could control my enthusiasm, he relaxed. He could again show me his yearnings to be loved, his anger when he was not loved. Our relationship grew stronger, and he began to share his dreams and fantasies. Like all patients, he swung back and forth—sometimes emotionally open, other times reverting to his mechanical way of coping. I tried my best to listen with empathy, not stimulate him too much, and Adam became more self-confident.

After three years of treatment, he was much more social in school, brought friends home, and showed a love for his parents, as if to say, "I forgive you." His parents thanked me for helping him become, as they put it, "so much more alive."

While their treatment helped them accommodate to Adam's changes, there is no doubt that his freedom to blast "Mr. Machine," then the world, then his parents openly, came from within Adam himself; it arose from his wish to survive emotionally. I had given him the chance to become aware of his fury, to express it, then to accept it quietly. Much of his energy had been bound up in repressing his anger. That energy was now free, and he could use it to study, to make friends, to accept his parents as they were.

Many years after therapy, Adam came to visit me. He told me he was majoring in physics at Yale University, intending to become a scientist. Though he related warmly to me, I detected a certain reserve. But compared to the autistic boy who would not even look at me, much less speak to me, and who erected a wall of building blocks to shut me out, I was more than satisfied—with Adam's work and with mine.

13

TERMINATION
When Analyst and Patient Take Leave of Each Other

One day a woman in her late twenties came for a consultation. She had the body and classic facial features of a model, but she wore a drab gray cotton dress. Lynn Michaels looked sorrowfully at me, gracefully lowered herself into the chair.

In a soft, seductive voice she said, "I'm very unhappy with my life. I'm only a secretary though I went to college, majored in literature. When my father died two years ago, he left me enough money so I don't worry about the next dollar. I have to work, though, because I go crazy when I just sit around the apartment."

She looked at me silently for a few moments, then said, "I've had several affairs but never wanted to get married. I seem to feel depressed when I'm alone. Sometimes I stammer when I feel nervous with a man. Do you think you can help me?"

I recalled this original impression of Lynn several years later when she was ready to end the analysis—what we call termination. By that time she had changed in many ways. Her drab clothes had been replaced by bright, fashionable dresses. Her stammering had ceased entirely. Instead of working as a low-paid secretary, she was the owner and director of a flourishing public relations firm. She was about to marry a reporter who wrote for a leading New York newspaper.

Much work took place in my office during the years of treatment, as Lynn swung between feeling I was the most wonderful man in the world and thinking I was the most despicable. At moments she fantasied maiming or murdering me; at other times she fantasied marrying me and bearing my children. Sometimes I emerged as her seductive but hostile father, at other times her masochistic mother who frequently appeared to Lynn as "quite stupid." On occasion she saw me as her older brother, toward whom she had mixed feelings of love and hate.

Just as Lynn experienced a range of feelings toward me and saw me as different people in her life, I made her different characters in my life and experienced varied feelings toward her. Most of the time I saw myself as Lynn's big brother, as I have tended to do with a number of young women I have treated. And just as I enjoyed helping my own sister grow and develop, I enjoyed helping Lynn grow and develop. Also, just as I felt jealous when my sister moved away from me and found her own man, I felt pangs of jealousy and envy at various times, particularly at the end of Lynn's analysis.

Occasionally I felt irritation with Lynn when, in fantasy, she made me the big brother she hated and wanted to demean. And from time to time I felt uncomfortable when she treated me like her provocative father or masochistic mother. But most of the time my feeling toward Lynn was a warm, loving one, and I could monitor both my sexual feelings toward her and my occasional irritation.

But now Lynn and I were talking about termination. How do analyst and patient decide when termination of an analysis is in order? There are probably as many opinions on this subject as there are analysts. It is one of the most controversial issues in psychoanalysis, and like many other controversies, it is shrouded in secrecy. Also, because very little research has been done on this subject, there have been few articles and books about termination.

When Freud was asked what his goals were in analyzing a patient, he replied tersely that he tried to enable him to *"lieben and arbeiten"* (to love and to work). But Freud was rather vague as to what he meant by loving and working. In his paper, "Analysis: Terminable and Interminable," he did talk about helping the patient master childish wishes to be loved and give up unrealistic fantasies about love. When a patient is able to do this, his emotional energy becomes available to love someone of the opposite sex and to work more productively.

But Freud's notions of love and work are so general that it is difficult to apply them as sound criteria by which to end an analysis. As you consider Freud's cases and those of some of his contemporaries, you get the impression he was frequently satisfied with "symptom relief"—if the patient's phobia, obsession, or psychosomatic symptom vanished, the analysis could be successfully terminated.

In considering the termination of an analysis, it is important to keep in mind that today's analysts are much more ambitious than Freud and his colleagues were. Nowadays they wish not only to help a patient give up symptoms but also to allow him to increase his self-esteem, improve his self-image, add to his pleasure in relationships, diminish his hatred, and help him cope more easily with frustration and disappointment.

This is a tall psychic order. As a result, analysis no longer takes only seven to ten months, as it did in Freud's day. Now it may run longer. Psychoanalysis has moved from a medical model of "symptom relief" to one in which the total character of the person is taken into consideration. One criterion for termination, which is used by many analysts, is based on Dr. Reuben Fine's concept of the "analytic ideal"—the patient is ready to end analysis when he is able to face and accept his hatred and love more maturely. He recognizes when it is realistic and appropriate to enjoy pleasure and when that pleasure may be self-destructive, as in alcoholism or promiscuity. The patient who is prepared to terminate analysis is creative, communicates readily, enjoys sex and his role in family and society.

This is, of course, an ideal toward which analysts and patients aspire. When Lynn and I considered her termination, she had achieved many of the components of the analytic ideal. She was more loving, enjoyed sex with her fiancé, had more self-esteem, and accepted herself and others more readily, no longer demanding perfection. Her creativity flowered as she moved from secretary to owner and director of her own public relations firm.

When Lynn and I began to discuss termination, her earlier conflicts reemerged, old anxieties reappeared. She again stammered at times, had difficulty concentrating on her work. She questioned her relationship with her future husband, even wondered whether analysis had been worthwhile.

Every patient with whom I have worked regresses at termination. This happens for two reasons. First, when a patient works with an analyst several sessions a week over a long period of time, he becomes very attached to the analyst. Part of the regression is the patient's way of saying, "I still need your help. Look at all my symptoms. You *can't* let me go." Second, all patients who enter analysis do so not only to relieve themselves of emotional suffering but also in the hope the analyst will gratify their childish wish for a parental figure. As illustrated throughout this book, every patient wants the analyst to adopt him as the favorite child, have sex with him, marry him, or engage in an affair with him. When the subject of termination is introduced, regardless of how successful the analysis has been, the child in the patient tries, perhaps for the last time, to get his every wish gratified.

Each patient responds to this difficult time in terms of his past. If separating from his mother's breast was traumatic, then separating from the analyst will be traumatic. If many separations throughout his life proved upsetting, then termination will be difficult. In effect, termination says to the patient, "You are on your own now."

How the patient responds to this realization depends on how he has handled independence previously. Patients are likely to find termination of analysis difficult if they experienced difficulty in toilet training, if their sexual curiosity was squelched, or if they were rushed to achieve prematurely in school.

The patient's reaction to termination in many ways reflects the story of his life and the way he viewed the analyst. The analyst responds similarly to termination. What kinds of separation took place in his life? What did each separation mean to him? How did he experience weaning, toilet training, sexual frustration?

But—and this is more important than any other factor—the termination process will be influenced by the analyst's feeling toward that particular patient. This area of analysis remains completely unexplored in the analytic literature, though one analyst did remark that termination begins the day the patient starts analysis. By that, he meant every session leads up to termination (the thought of it is always there, albeit in the unconscious at times) and contains in it the essence of whether termination will be easy or hard for both patient and analyst. One of the goals of analysis is to help the patient accept termination with as little pain as possible.

For me, termination has always been one of the most difficult parts of my job. How I experience termination with my patients relates to the story of my life. During my first twenty-one years I lived in eighteen different houses in half a dozen cities in Canada and the United States. As a result of all that moving, I still find separation difficult. Each time I face termination, I think of giving up close friends, moving away from a familiar neighborhood, saying good-bye to relatives, classmates, teachers. Separation conjures up memories of being pushed prematurely to take on new responsibilities. As a reaction, I have tended to be cautious about terminating an analysis. If I have erred, it has been on the side of keeping a patient who might have been able to leave earlier. Though my own analyst never said so, I have the feeling he took into consideration my premature weaning and toilet training and my many changes of residence, and thus was in no hurry to let me go.

For years I felt devastated when I saw a patient grow and develop, then regress at termination. I would start to react like the child who had disappointed his parents. Now, as I ended Lynn's analysis, all of these factors were at work. When her symptoms returned, my own childhood memories began to stir. I could hear the voice of my father asking, "Why didn't you get all A's?" I still felt I had to try for that elusive "perfection."

An ex-patient may always have inside him the residue of old conflicts. This residue will get stirred up occasionally throughout his life, but he will now have much more mastery over those old conflicts, because he is conscious of them. In much the same way, all analysts, I believe, relive in part their ancient conflicts and losses at each termination.

As Lynn's symptoms returned and she began to berate me, I felt tinges of the old conflicts. At one session she displayed anger at my refusal to marry her, or adopt her, and I recalled my sister crying at my wedding and my unhappiness when I saw her distress. Since in fantasy I had at times made Lynn my younger sister, I had to face separations and losses that involved my relationship with my sister. As Lynn discharged her anger and tried once again, albeit briefly, to persuade me to have sex with her or live with her, then realized her fantasies were hopeless, she grew closer to her fiancé; they set a wedding date near the day of termination.

While I did not show approval or disapproval of Lynn's getting married at any point, I felt toward her the way I felt when my sister married. In one session, as Lynn was excitedly describing her wedding plans, I developed a headache, not common for me during analytic work. I recalled having had a headache while flying from New York to Ann Arbor to attend my sister's wedding.

Just as I felt some anger at giving up my sister to another man, I now experienced a resurgence of anger as I worked toward termination with Lynn. By that time I had said goodbye to a number of young women patients, and I recalled times when, for one reason or another, my unwillingness to let a patient go became apparent. It is easy, of course, for an analyst to justify the continuation of an analysis. No human being can achieve the analytic "ideal," and fantasies, wishes, and acts can often be analyzed in more depth and breadth. The unconscious, like a vast ocean of memories, seems to have no bottom.

Each phase of Lynn's analysis reemerged during the six months of termination. Just as she relived old losses, old conflicts, I found myself reexperiencing feelings I'd had toward her during different phases of her analysis. I also experienced former losses and conflicts.

Because of Lynn's intense closeness to her father, an important part of her analysis was an attempt to recapture that relationship through me. As a symbiosis-craver myself,

I had to work in a cautious way whenever she told me how much she loved me, how intelligent and charming I was, how no man could in any way be my equal. These were flattering comments to hear from an attractive, bright young woman, and I had to remind myself that it was my job not to gratify her wish, but to help her renounce and understand her proclamation of love. I also worked hard to monitor my wish to compete with Lynn's father and, of course, with my own father. Such yearnings do not die; you only learn to make them conscious, accept them, handle them more easily.

Termination may be like the death, or the half-death perhaps, of a loved one. For Lynn, memories of her father reemerged, and she again mourned his death, just as I remourned my father's death. It is one thing to help a patient renounce a childish wish for a father as the relationship between patient and analyst continues. But when that relationship ends, both parties, if they are emotionally honest, feel a new loss and sadness—a real loss based on their real relationship in the present. The patient is grateful for the analyst's help in facing the inner self; the analyst feels proud of having helped the patient reduce his suffering and live more happily.

Freud differentiated between "mourning" and "melancholia," pointing out that the person who mourns, though he may have had mixed feelings about the "dear departed," basically loved him. But in melancholia, hate predominates over love, and the mourner becomes agitated, depressed, and unhappy. When I see signs of melancholia at termination, either in myself or in the patient, I know some conflicts remain unresolved.

I felt somewhat melancholy, as did Lynn, when we talked for the last time about my being her fantasied father. I explained that both of us were reexperiencing the death of a fantasy—there would be no Garden of Eden for either of us, and we had to renounce the paradise we had hoped to regain.

My recognition of my irritation at not having had the perfect father or the perfect analyst helped me to help Lynn give me up—give up the fantasy in which I could be her father, and move toward a realistic relationship with her fiancé.

Because Lynn could now see that I possessed both strengths and limitations, she was ready for termination. One of the goals of analysis is to help the patient see the analyst realistically. When he is no longer idealized, no longer viewed as the provider of gratification, the patient can accept reality with more equanimity.

In addition to giving up her idealized father, Lynn had to renounce her deep anger toward her mother. Because her mother was not a giving woman, Lynn had made her father into both father and mother. It was important during her analysis to help her get in touch with the part of herself that yearned to be emotionally nurtured in a tender way by a man who served as a mother substitute.

During her analysis she was able to vent her rage at her emotionally unavailable mother. As her tears flowed, she could experience me as the mother who cared, and her life improved dramatically. At this time her appearance changed, her self-esteem increased, and her body image became modified—she started to look at herself as an attractive woman rather than as a discarded object for which her father had no use. She realized both men and women could love her, and with this newfound confidence she could set forth on a new and far more challenging professional life.

But now Lynn wondered how she would get along without the loving mother she had found in me. We spent many analytic hours talking about her feeling that as long as I was in her life all went well. At one point she referred to me as her spinal cord. She said as long as she was attached to me she could feel capable and confident but without her "spinal cord" she would fall apart.

I could identify with Lynn as she lamented her loss, because I had felt the same way when my analysis was ending. An analyst is like a parent: in his presence the patient feels strengthened. Therefore the loss of the analyst may be terrifying or, at the very least, an acute deprivation. When you cling to another person, whether it be analyst, spouse, or friend, you are showing your unwillingness to give up the role of the infant who is unable to face the anger that accompanies any form of emotional weaning.

I had to help Lynn accept the fact that I could not be the symbiotic mother she had always craved. Analysts and patients may sometimes forget that the analyst can never be a permanent parental substitute. He can only be a catalyst, helping the patient face childish hungers and childish resentments in an accepting atmosphere.

The analyst's goal is to help the patient accept the fact that wishing to continue to be a child is an illusion. Hating parents and others for not gratifying the yearnings of childhood is futile.

Although I empathized with Lynn's anger, I did not indulge her childish wish to remain with me. Slowly she adopted my point of view which, as much as possible, represented reality. In this reality, the patient understands that there are many pleasures in life to be enjoyed, but he cannot remain an infant at the breast or a child in bed with his parents. In this reality, life offers pleasures, but it also contains frustrations and disappointments.

When Lynn's disappointment receded, I knew she was ready to set a date for termination. She began to grow close once again to her fiancé and more involved in her professional life. She felt and acted like the young person who can say good-bye to parents and achieve a separation that is not hostile or debilitating emotionally but necessary for a strong sense of identity.

When an analysis ends, anxieties and conflicts do not disappear like puffs of smoke. Anxieties are part of living; the patient will feel some realistic anxiety at times, but his anxiety over unreal fantasies will have vanished. Conflict, like anxiety, is an inherent part of life. We experience it when we are forced to make a difficult decision or give up a pleasure. We have to continue to monitor our childish impulses and rages. Self-analysis always continues after formal analysis ends.

Like all patients, Lynn had learned a new way of coping with her anxieties and conflicts. She would continue arriving at insights, facing her buried memories and fantasies. Analysis helps patients become more at home with their unconscious. The unconscious is no longer forbidden terrain that frightens them, keeps them from exploring new realms of the mind.

Each time I have a last session with a patient, I think of what my teacher, Theodor Reik, once said. He told us about the last time he saw Freud, who had been his analyst. He described how Freud had put his arm around him, then said, as his last good-bye: "People need not be glued together when they belong together."

For a short while, during analysis, patient and analyst are glued together. Neither of thom will ever forget the importance of that relationship. What happened in the closed room to enable the patient to live more in peace with himself and the world will remain forever etched on their minds.

217

EPILOGUE

When I was thirteen I moved with my parents and sister from Montreal to New Rochelle, New York. Living in a new and faraway town was difficult for me, especially during the first few months. I acutely missed my extended family and my friends. And many of my peers ridiculed me because of my Canadian accent and overly polite, sometimes ingratiating, demeanor with teachers.

To compound these difficulties, I was placed in the sophomore class, where the other students were two to three years older than I. Depressed, socially isolated, and angry, I sought solace at the local synagogue. There I felt emotionally nourished and enriched as I joined the congregants in singing Hebrew melodies.

At the synagogue in the row in front of me sat the internationally famous Metropolitan Opera tenor, Jan Peerce. To my surprise and joy, from the moment I met him Mr. Peerce always greeted me warmly. Once or twice he even asked me to sit next to him so we could sing together. My self-esteem rose. In contrast to my teachers and fellow students who barely tolerated me, Jan Peerce offered warmth, compassion, and sincerity. In those days I told myself more than once, "If this famous man is so nice to me, I must be acceptable."

My experience with Jan Peerce and other benign parental figures influenced my choosing psychoanalysis as a profession. It slowly dawned on me that receiving acceptance, compassion, and genuine understanding could reduce rage, self-hatred, and depression. I realized these qualities in a helping person could raise self-esteem and self-confidence in those who needed it, sometimes desperately.

For me, nothing quite surpasses the exhilarating feeling of being loved and understood, particularly by a person I can love and respect. People like Jan Peerce, by virtue of their outstanding achievements, could hold themselves aloof, but they prefer to mingle with fellow members of the human race. These people say through words and deeds, "We are all more human than otherwise," the belief of Dr. Harry Stack Sullivan.

Because I realized, with much conviction early in life, that it was uplifting to receive love, understanding, and compassion, I wanted to make a living offering these vital emotional nutrients to others. At nineteen, for a philosophy class at New York University, I had to write a paper entitled "The Three Principles That Guide My Life." I listed these three principles: my strong yearning for love, my thirst for knowledge, and my deep desire to provide love and knowledge to those who would accept it. By nineteen, in other words, I had the wish to become a psychoanalyst.

I believe men and women choose psychoanalysis as a career after an experience similar to the one I had with Jan Peerce. A number of analysts have told me they first thought of training for therapeutic work after being patients in psychotherapy and deriving many benefits from their own analyses.

I hope this book shows the psychoanalyst as first and foremost a human being with his own loves, hates, joys, sufferings, conflicts, biases, and ambivalences. I have emphasized that, in order to do successful therapeutic work, the analyst must compassionately identify with his patient, feel the patient's agonies and conflicts within himself.

I have further attempted to show that an analyst, even if he has undergone the finest training in the world, loses his empathic stance, lessening his effectiveness, if he resists seeing himself as similar to his patient. The cases I have presented attest to this: when I worked with a homosexual, I had to cope with my own homosexual fantasies and conflicts; when I was the recipient of erotic fantasies from an attractive woman, I had to face my own feelings of sexual arousal and, in addition, face the "woman" in me that wanted love from a man; when a patient spewed hatred I had to confront my own hatred. The same was true with other feelings: when my patients expressed envy, revenge, greed, competition, or jealousy, I had to face these emotions in myself. I have tried to point out that when I did not face those parts of myself which patients were talking about in themselves, a stalemate occurred or the therapy failed altogether.

Psychoanalysts believe that what sustains people's unhappiness is that they bring unhappy experiences with parents and siblings of childhood into the present. They see their bosses as their authoritarian fathers of the past. They turn their spouses into the earlier emotionally engulfing mother. They imagine their children as rivalrous siblings. They fantasy friends and colleagues as parents and other family members with whom they had conflicted relationships.

Most psychoanalytic work involves studying how the patient distorts the analyst, making him into figures of the patient's past or unacceptable parts of the patient's own psyche. To help a patient become more loving and less hateful, more realistic and less involved in daydreams and distortions, more communicative, more feeling, more creative, better able to play a significant role in the family and in society, the analyst must constantly study how he sees the patient as a figure of his past or an unacceptable part of his own psyche.

Freud said, "Every psychoanalytic treatment is an attempt to free repressed love." Virtually all analysts would agree with that statement. However, to free love and reduce hate, the patient must experience the analyst as a human being who has endured most of the conflicts the patient brings to the couch.

One of the most difficult dimensions of being a psychoanalyst is to recognize over and over again that though you are behind the couch, you are essentially a mortal who must constantly struggle to master your own childish and erotic and aggressive responses. I have found that those analysts who truly see themselves as very similar to their patients enjoy their work much more than those who consider their patients apart from them. These are the analysts who can constantly learn from their patients and from time to time use them as "consultants."

The analyst who accepts his essential humanness will be surprised from time to time, because he acknowledges he does not possess all the answers and must learn many of them from his patients.

I have tried in this book to share with the reader how I experienced my patients—when I turned them into my exacting father or my ambivalent mother or my envied sister. In my family of origin I experienced many agonies and many ecstasies. I derived strengths from my parents and sister—a sense of responsibility, a sense of humor, and common sense, to name a few positives. I also developed some neurotic ways of coping—overambitiousness, obsessive-compulsiveness, and overzealousness, to name a few negatives.

All this makes me similar to my patients as I, too, struggle to make my life more enjoyable, to love others more, to hate less and to like myself as much as is reasonable. I trust this makes me a more effective and a more compassionate psychoanalyst.